Lecture Notes
in Business Information Processing 35

Olly Gotel   Mathai Joseph
Bertrand Meyer (Eds.)

Software Engineering Approaches for Offshore and Outsourced Development

Third International Conference, SEAFOOD 2009
Zurich, Switzerland, July 2-3, 2009
Proceedings

 Springer

Volume Editors

Olly Gotel
Pace University
New York City, NY 10038, USA
E-mail: ogotel@pace.edu

Mathai Joseph
Tata Consultancy Services
Pune 411 001, India
E-mail: m.joseph@tcs.com

Bertrand Meyer
ETH Zurich
Department of Computer Science
8092 Zurich, Switzerland
E-mail: Bertrand.Meyer@inf.ethz.ch

Library of Congress Control Number: 2009929830

ACM Computing Classification (1998): D.2, K.6, K.4.2, J.1

ISSN   1865-1348
ISBN-10   3-642-02986-8 Springer Berlin Heidelberg New York
ISBN-13   978-3-642-02986-8 Springer Berlin Heidelberg New York

springer.com

© Springer-Verlag Berlin Heidelberg 2009
Printed in Germany

Typesetting: Camera-ready by author, data conversion by Scientific Publishing Services, Chennai, India
Printed on acid-free paper   SPIN: 12717293   06/3180   5 4 3 2 1 0

Preface
SEAFOOD 2009: Enabling Global Partnerships to Deliver on Business Needs

Companies have been outsourcing areas of software development work for many years, either because of the engineering challenges or because the outsourced aspect is not central to their core business. A profound transformation has been affecting this model over recent years: a massive transfer of development activities from the USA and Europe to a skilled labor force in service-providing countries. This transformation has been driven by the demands of a global business climate seeking to increase the value delivery of IT investment. However, the ability to realize this value can prove problematic in practice. Of particular concern are the hidden costs of globally distributed models of working, such as understanding and communicating the true business needs across organizational and cultural boundaries.

To address such issues, offshore outsourcing requires different support from in-house development and this means adapting familiar techniques, processes and tools to this setting, as well as perhaps creating innovative new ones. Coupled with this industry transformation there is hence a pressing need to re-examine those software engineering approaches that either facilitate or impede this model of working. With an inevitable focus on the economy in 2009, business decisions regarding the sourcing of software development projects will come under close scrutiny. It will become increasingly critical to design global partnerships that both clarify cost/benefits and enable delivery on business needs.

SEAFOOD 2009, the Third International Conference on Software Engineering Approaches for Offshore and Outsourced Development, was held at ETH Zürich during July 2–3, 2009. Bertrand Meyer and Mathai Joseph established the SEAFOOD series of conferences in 2007 in an attempt to not only bring software engineering to outsourcing but also to bring outsourcing into the collective consciousness of the software engineering community. SEAFOOD seeks to provide an opportunity for participants from academia and industry to present and discuss experiences, ideas and proposals related to this topic.

Reflecting the global nature of offshore outsourcing, SEAFOOD 2009 received submissions from Australia, Bangladesh, Brazil, China, Denmark, Finland, Germany, India, Italy, Japan, Switzerland, The Philippines, Thailand and the USA. The 12 articles in this volume were selected for presentation and discussion. These include 9 papers from industry (5 full papers and 4 short position papers) and 3 full research papers from academia. The conference program also included two keynote presentations and the abstracts are contained in this volume: "Decentralized Software Development: Pitfalls and Challenges," delivered by Carlo Ghezzi, Politecnico di Milano, Italy; and "An Empiricist View of

Managing Globally Distributed Software Development," delivered by Narayan Ramasubbu, Singapore Management University, Singapore. The conference program was supplemented by an industry panel discussion organized by David Michael of United Business Media on the theme of "Software Engineering Practices to Ensure Success in a Multi-country Environment." The conference site at http://seafood.ethz.ch includes information on this conference, as well as on past and future SEAFOOD events.

Many people contributed to SEAFOOD 2009. In particular, Martin Nordio played a central role throughout the organization of the conference, assisting with the program logistics, local arrangements and preparation of this volume. We thank the industry and education Program Chairs, David Michael and Christelle Scharff for their attention to the industry and education submissions. We also thank the entire Program Committee for their timely work in reviewing submissions and Patrick Mäder for attending to publicity. SEAFOOD 2009 was co-located with TOOLS 2009 and we are further grateful to Claudia Günthart for assisting with the local arrangements.

May 2009   Olly Gotel
                                              Mathai Joseph
                                             Bertrand Meyer

Conference Organization

Program Chairs

Bertrand Meyer   ETH Zürich, Switzerland – General Co-chair
Mathai Joseph   Tata Consultancy Services, India – General
     Co-chair
Olly Gotel   Pace University, New York City, USA –
     Program Chair

Organizing Committee

David Michael   United Business Media, USA – Industry Track
Christelle Scharff   Pace University, USA – Education Track
Patrick Mäder   Ilmenau Technical University, Germany –
     Publicity

Program Committee

Pamela Abbott   Brunel University, UK
Kay Berkling   Inline Internet Online GmbH, Germany
Manfred Broy   Technische Universität München, Germany
Val Casey   Bournemouth University, UK
Oliver Creighton   Siemens AG, Germany
Jean-Pierre Corriveau   Carleton University, Canada
Al Davis   University of Colorado and The Davis
     Company, USA
Barry Dwolatzky   Wits University, South Africa
Patricia Ensworth   Harborlight Management Services, USA
Samuel Fricker   University of Zürich and
     FUCHS-INFORMATIK AG, Switzerland
Don Gause   SUNY Binghamton and Savile Row, LLC,
     USA
Matt Ganis   IBM Hawthorne, USA
Victor Gergel   University of Nizhni Novgorod, Russia
Tony Gorschek   Blekinge Institute of Technology, Sweden
Amar Gupta   University of Arizona, USA
David Klappholz   Stevens Institute of Technology, USA
Vidya Kulkarni   University of Delhi, India
Vinay Kulkarni   Tata Research Development and Design
     Centre, India
Liz Q. Li   Motorola Inc., USA

Christine Mingins   ucube, Australia
Cornelius Ncube   Bournemouth University, UK
Uolevi Nikula   Lappeenranta University of Technology,
        Finland
Dragutin Petkovic   San Francisco State University, USA
Moniphal Say   Institute of Technology of Cambodia,
        Cambodia
Thanwadee Sunetnanta Mahidol University, Thailand
Gary Thompson   Sun Microsystems and San Francisco State
        University, USA
Rainer Todtenhoefer   University of Applied Sciences Fulda,
        Germany
Hiroshi Tsuji   Osaka Prefecture University, Japan
Ye Yang   Institute of Software Chinese Academy of
        Sciences, China
Yunwen Ye   Software Research Associates, Inc., Japan
Jianjun Zhao   Shanghai Jiao Tong University, China

Local Organization

Martin Nordio   ETH Zürich, Switzerland
Claudia Günthart   ETH Zürich, Switzerland

Table of Contents

Strategic Concerns and Technologies

Communication and Specification

Decentralized Software Development: Pitfalls and Challenges

Carlo Ghezzi

Politecnico di Milano, Italy
carlo.ghezzi@polimi.it

Abstract. The talk discusses different three main threads through which monolithic and centralized software development became increasingly distributed and decentralized. One is off-shoring, in which geographically distributed teams cooperate in the development of an application. Another is component-based software development, in which two separate development cycles interact: development of component and development of the composite. A third thread is software-as-service, in which the two main stakeholders (service provider and the service client) continue to interact at run time. Each of these threads has its own potential advantages over traditional software development, but also raises fundamental concerns. The talk discusses how they stress some of the conceptually difficult aspects of software development and how they introduce new problems and difficulties that did not exist before.

Short Biography

Carlo Ghezzi is a Professor and Chair of Software Engineering at Politecnico di Milano. He is the Rectors Delegate for research. In the past, he has been a member of the Academic Senate and a Member of the Board of Governors of Politecnico. He also held positions as Department Chair, Head of the PhD Program and Head of consiglio di corso di laurea. He has also been affiliated with: Universit di Padova, University of California at Los Angeles, University of North Carolina at Chapel Hill, University of California at Santa Barbara (USA), Escuela Superior Latino-Americana de Informatica (Argentina), Technical University of Vienna and University of Klagenfurt (Austria), University of Lugano (Switzerland).

He is a Fellow of the ACM (citation: Numerous research contributions from compiler theory to real-time systems to software processes. A strong contributor to the software engineering community in Europe and worldwide.) and Fellow of the IEEE (citation: Contributions to programming languages and software engineering). He was awarded the ACM SIGSOFT Distinguished Service Award. He is a member of the Academy of Sciences. He has been a member of several governmental committees and was the Italian representative in the EU Information Technology Committee (Esprit Programme) during the 4th Framework Programme. He has been on the board of several international research projects and institutions in Europe, Japan, and the USA.

O. Gotel, M. Joseph, and B. Meyer (Eds.): SEAFOOD 2009, LNBIP 35, pp. 1–2, 2009.

He is a regular member of the program committee of flagship conferences of the software engineering field, such as the International Conference on Software Engineering and Foundations of Software Engineering/ European Software Engineering Conference, for which he also served as Program and General Chair. He has been General Chair of the International Conference on Service Oriented Computing (ICSOC 2006, Chicago, USA). He has been the Editor in Chief of the ACM Transactions on Software Engineering and Methodology and Associate Editor of IEEE Transactions on Software Engineering. He is currently an Associate Editor of Science of Computer Programming (Elsevier), Service Oriented Computing and Applications (Springer), and Software Process Improvement and Practice (J. Wiley and Sons).

Carlo Ghezzis research has been focusing on different aspects of software engineering and programming languages. Currently, he is active in the area of software architectures, especially evolvable and distributed software architectures for ubiquitous and pervasive computer applications. He co-authored over 150 papers, almost all of which are published internationally, and 8 books. He coordinated several national and international (EU funded) research projects. He has been a recipient of an ERC Advanced Research Grant in 2008.

An Empiricist View of Managing Globally Distributed Software Development

Narayan Ramasubbu

Singapore Management University, Singapore
nramasub@smu.edu.sg

Abstract. Software Engineering research is still catching up with the explosive growth in the adoption and proliferation of distributed software development in its many forms. In this talk, I will present the research roadmap I, as an empirical researcher, had taken to investigate distributed software development, and will highlight the key findings and inferences from my exploration. Drawing evidence from more than two hundred large scale distributed software development projects that I had observed in the past five years, I will discuss the challenges faced by distributed software teams along with the way these teams (and their organizations) have responded to the challenges. I will also share my views on the existing gaps, both theoretical and empirical, in software engineering economics literature that need to be bridged to further our understanding of distributed software development. These gaps specifically relate to how software engineering researchers and practitioners accommodate distributedness in project planning, execution, control and reflection activities. Overall, my discussions will call for a new set of governance schemes specifically suited for distributed software development projects, and will lay out a roadmap for empirical software engineers to build one.

Short Biography

Narayan Ramasubbu is an assistant professor at the School of Information Systems at the Singapore Management University. He has a Ph.D. in Business Administration from the University of Michigan, Ann Arbor, and an Electronics and Telecommunications Engineering degree from Bharathiyar University, India. Prior to pursuing the Ph.D., he was a senior developer and product management specialist, first at CGI Inc. and then at SAP AG. His research focuses on software engineering economics, distributed software product development, and software product standardization and customization. His research statement and projects can be viewed at http://www.sis.smu.edu.sg/faculty/infosys/nramasub.asp.

O. Gotel, M. Joseph, and B. Meyer (Eds.): SEAFOOD 2009, LNBIP 35, p. 3, 2009.

IBM Industry Practice: Challenges in Offshore Software Development from a Global Delivery Center

Ilario Musio

IBM
ilario.musio@ch.ibm.com
http://www.ibm.com

Abstract. Offshore software development has greatly influenced competitiveness among IT companies in the last decade. Despite the fact that there are matured and developed offshoring methodologies, there is an ongoing tendency to look for new ways of improving them. Major IT corporations successfully rely on their offshore delivery centers for bridging the gap between communication and infrastructure boundaries. However, projects tend to fail, so problems have to be considered that arise between on- and offshore parts within the same corporation. Based on seven case studies from the industry, this paper describes experiences and challenges faced during the execution of offshore application development between IBM Switzerland and IBM India. Additionally, approaches on how they can be solved are proposed.

Keywords: offshore insourcing, global delivery, offshoring, India, industry practice.

1 Introduction

The IT industry is undergoing a great change in how software is developed. With the world getting flatter, faster and smarter, more and more ideas arise on how to execute business in a way to benefit economically and technically. Offshore outsourcing is one such solution multinational IT corporations have turned to for cutting development costs to remain competitive. Since distributed projects started to fail [13], companies and researchers have been searching for new ways to improve the function of globally distributed teams [2]. One major investment has been the construction of global delivery centers spread all over the world, especially in emerging countries such as India. These centers serve as outsourcing partners with the advantage of being within the same corporation [4].

The main benefits are:

- Shorter project set-up times due to internal contracting
- Standard infrastructure and communication channels
- Consistent methodologies and processes
- Increased security and confidentiality
- Protection of proprietary knowledge.

O. Gotel, M. Joseph, and B. Meyer (Eds.): SEAFOOD 2009, LNBIP 35, pp. 4–13, 2009.

However, achieving these benefits in practice can be challenging. The constantly changing IT environment brings about new problems that must each be overcome.

2   The Global Delivery India Program

IBM operates global delivery centers in eight countries across four continents. The largest division is located in India, where approximately 60,000 people are employed.

While IBM Switzerland has been delivering offshore projects to India for many years, collaboration between shores continues to be a challenge. In response, it started the *Global Delivery India* program [19]. Ten Swiss application developers were sent to India in 2007. They were each assigned to different offshore projects for a year, where they worked as members of the development teams. The goal of the program was to gain experience within a globally distributed software development team, identify collaboration barriers between shores and define best practices for a globally integrated software delivery methodology.

Taking part in this program gave participants the opportunity to view the distributed software engineering process from the offshore team's point of view. It gave them a first-hand look at how Indian colleagues approach and execute software development, as well as the way in which the project deals with cultural differences, distributed communication strategies, and offshore project management.

Traditionally, IBM uses its corporation-wide methodologies to manage software development projects. Its methods and processes are executed thoroughly and are being constantly improved. However, before those methodologies can be adapted for distributed projects, a number of questions must first be answered:

– Where do the methodologies currently being applied fail?
– How can those methodologies be efficiently applied on offshore projects?
– What kind of problems go undetected in offshore software development projects, and how can they be solved?
– At what points in the project lifecycle do coordination and communication issues arise?

This paper discusses the experiences and lessons learned during the *Global Delivery India* program. All experiences are based on qualitative assessments on seven different global delivery case studies, as well as surveys involving the program participants, project managers, and other stakeholders on both shores in Europe and India. The applied survey methodology is described in more detail in section 4.

The following sections describe experiences that directly affected the execution of the offshore projects. Recommended approaches are presented in separate subsections.

3　Experiences

3.1　Cultural Diversity

Cultural differences can impede a smooth collaboration. Messages can be interpreted differently by different cultures which can lead to misunderstandings and confusion [8].

Especially during the starting phases of the case study projects, several cultural misunderstandings were experienced. A typical misunderstanding is the different perception of the word "Yes." An Indian "Yes" may not only mean "I agree," but could also mean "I understand what you are saying, but I do not agree with you." [18]. This led to ambiguous perceptions on e.g., the completeness of a work unit or to wrongly interpreted requirements.

Being aware of such cultural misconceptions is the basic rule for a successful offshore project [3].

Recommended Approach: Cultural Awareness Education. Take steps to ensure the entire team, on- and offshore, is aware of the cultural differences between the originating country and India, regardless of how responsibilities are divided within the project. Special attention must be given to team members that will directly interact with the other shore or with the client. This might consist of awareness classroom courses with focus on cultural conflicts that have a direct impact on intercultural collaboration [10], [7].

In any case, the importance of cultural awareness must not be underestimated. If classroom training courses are not possible, material describing at least the basic cultural differences should be prepared and distributed among the onsite and offshore practitioners for them to study in the project's initial phase.

3.2　Workforce Capability

The success of a global delivery project ultimately depends on an involved workforce. Methodologies and processes may be optimal, but the real challenge can be finding engineers with the required skills.

It can be difficult to find practitioners with many years of experience in a specific field or development environment in India. With the constantly growing technology market in India, there is a high staff turnover within IT companies. Indian IT specialists can readily find another job with a better salary, which causes great volatility in IT teams, making frequent hiring processes and university recruiting events a necessity. The program revealed that many hiring processes do not always meet European standards. Observations showed that the majority of new hires did not have the expected technical knowledge. This is due to the fact that university hires can come from fields of study that are unrelated to IT.

Recommended Approach: Monitor Practitioner Hiring Process. It is important to verify each practitioner's skill set, especially for newly set up projects.

Review all practitioners hired offshore and make sure to assemble a skillful and competent team. Delegating of hiring processes to an offshore representative should be kept to a minimum, as skill requirement concepts can vary among different societies. This is especially important when new hires join a team.

When hiring, do not rely solely on résumés and recommendation letters. Phone interviews should be the preferred hiring method. Candidates should be assessed on the required skills before being considered for the position. If training is required prior to joining a team, verify that the candidate successfully completed the training.

3.3 Methodologies

Major software corporations use their own methodologies and processes for guiding and managing software projects e.g., Rational Unified Process, XP, Agile, SCRUM, etc. These methodologies are being adapted for offshore outsourcing [11], [6].

As experiences from the case studies revealed, it is crucial for the success of the project that everyone is aware of the in-house processes and tools.

Awareness of standard methods helps all practitioners clearly understand their roles within the project and provides a common vocabulary based on clear definitions. Those advantages improve productivity by reducing ambiguity which enhances effective project execution.

Recommended Approach: Provide Information about Methodology. Choose a well-defined methodology, and propagate it not only to the onsite project managers, architects, and developers, but to the entire offshore team as well. The methodology provides a bigger picture, and it allows offshore practitioners to proactively contribute to the project.

3.4 Creativity

Work tasks and deliverables in which creativity and innovation are important should not be sent offshore [12]. Innovation occurs when programmers come up with creative ideas while they are working. If the offshore teams do not have creative programmers, potential innovation might be lost in the project.

Some deliverables in particular require the client to be close at hand, so as to involve them early on and avoid unnecessary acceptance iterations.

In one of the case studies, the graphical unit interface module was developed offshore. Though the functionality was complete, the screen arrangement did not meet the client's expectations. This led to additional acceptance iterations that could have been avoided.

Recommended Approach: Keep Creative Work Units. Examples of creative and innovative deliverables are e.g., Graphical Unit Interface screens, interaction process definitions and other Human-Computer interaction models.

Those deliverables should be developed on site and not assigned to the offshore team to avoid prolonging the communication process.

Nevertheless, promote innovation and creativity in the offshore team. Let the Indian colleagues perform autonomously and motivate them to suggest improvements. After a tighter relationship is built and the Indian team gets to know the client better, increasingly creative tasks can be sent offshore.

3.5   Productivity

Labor productivity can be measured as the amount of productive work during a specific amount of time. As distractions increase, productivity decreases. Observations from the case studies showed that during Indian social and cultural events productivity falls below normal levels. This was observed e.g., during the Diwali festivities in October, during the December and January "wedding season", or during political strikes in unstable cities. Differences in productivity between the seasons were also observed e.g., heavy rain impedes many people from going to the office, due to unstable transit systems.

Recommended Approach: Monitor Productivity. In traditional schedule and milestone management, festivities are usually taken into consideration. Make sure to keep the Indian holiday calendar in mind, as described above.

Completion of detailed activity reports by practitioners should also be required in order to better assess their activities. Verify that all practitioners record their activities using an adequate level of detail.

An online hour tracking tool might be introduced and applied, where practitioners record their activities on a daily basis.

3.6   Infrastructure and Organizational Tools

Despite having a company-wide infrastructure, it is not used equally everywhere. In most of the case study projects it was shown that calendar and scheduling systems were not being used correctly. There were many ad hoc meetings and calls, making advance planning difficult and causing appointment overlaps, poorly organized meeting room reservations, etc.

Development frameworks were also used unevenly. The use of commonly configured development environments is essential in order to plan, build, and trace all involved deliverables [16].

Recommended Approach: Increase Adherence to Organizational Procedures. Make sure the company-wide calendar is used appropriately for meetings, calls, social events, and even private appointments. If necessary, conduct training sessions, especially for newly hired personnel.

3.7   Communication

Communication problems are a major cause of offshore project failures. Issues have been described in many studies and academic researches [11]. Barriers to interaction between offshore and onsite team must be kept to a minimum. Well-structured and continuous communication among team members improves performance and makes project success more likely [9], [5].

Recommended Approach: Emphasize Communication Strategies. Ensure the usage of both synchronous and asynchronous communication tools [14]. Experiences from the case studies showed clear improvement in collaboration efficiency when using asynchronous communication tools, such as Instant Messengers or online collaboration tools. However, all team members must commit to using the chosen tool regularly [15].

Create email distribution lists, as well as instant messenger groups that include onshore and offshore team members. Designate offshore and onsite administrators to keep the lists updated. Let the offshore team know that any member on the onsite team will be available for queries and questions through instant messenger.

At the same time, schedule weekly phone calls and plan face-to-face visits to develop trust and build a healthy relationship. This makes it much easier to maintain a virtual team.

3.8 Meetings and Attentiveness

In a distributed environment, meetings between onsite and offshore team are conducted mainly by telephone.

It was observed that during phone calls some participants might switch off the microphone and then gradually become less attentive.

Recommended Approach: Conduct Effective Meetings. Choose video conferences over phone calls or chats wherever possible. Using webcams over the Internet avoids costs of expensive video conference systems.

Always remind the attendees to switch off their mobile phones during meetings, as it is not uncommon in India for a phone to ring in the middle of a meeting.

It is a good practice to prepare an agenda for the meeting in order that everyone involved is aware of the planned discussion points [14]. This document can then be transcribed into the meeting's minutes. Require the minutes to be signed off, to ensure that all parties have fully understood and agreed with the decisions made.

3.9 Uncertainty and Ambiguity

Differences among cultures imply different ways of interaction between onsite and offshore team members. In certain cultures, it can be considered impolite to directly disagree with someone, while in another culture people might speak more plainly [8].

In the Indian culture communication is less direct than in Western countries. It was observed that Indian team members were asking fewer questions than their Swiss counterparts. This led to misunderstandings, since for the onsite team, asking no questions implied that a given task was fully understood.

Recommended Approach: Avoid Uncertainty. Always encourage the Indian team to ask questions whenever in doubt.

In order to improve comprehensibility, write detailed technique and process definition documents while always remembering the cultural factors described in section 3.1. Make sure the offshore team understands the documentation, and ask questions to verify their understanding. Properly translate all documents before sending them offshore.

It is essential to keep an open-minded attitude toward the other culture and its implicit communication.

3.10 Deadlines

Deadlines delineate the project boundaries and form a basis for milestone management. Unfortunately, different cultures perceive deadlines differently. In Switzerland, adhering to deadlines goes without saying, while Indian colleagues tend to be more flexible in managing their time. They may not view a deadline as imperative unless its importance has been highlighted explicitly.

Furthermore, many Hindi speakers use the same expression for the following two sentences: "I will do it" and "I shall/might do it." Using this expression makes unclear whether it will actually be done or not. When this expression is used, be sure to verify the true meaning that lies behind it.

Recommended Approach: Enforce Deadline Adherence. Deadlines should be deliberately set early e.g., by one or two days. Always include a precise target time, e.g., "until June 27th, 5:00 p.m. CET." Additionally, be sure to frequently ask about the progress being made and whether the current deadline is still realistic.

3.11 Documentation and Knowledge Transfer

Knowledge transfer is critical in any kind of transition e.g., project hand-over or new people joining a team. Due to the high staff turnover in India, offshore teams can be very volatile and knowledge transfer becomes crucial. Three out of seven case study projects had poor or no documentation at all. New team members, especially new hires, needed more time to become acquainted with the project. This led to unexpected delays, which is a major risk in offshore projects [1].

Recommended Approach: Improve Documentation. Follow the guidelines below to create and maintain stable documentation:

- Create architectural documents describing implemented modules
- Require documentation for every decision and assumption taken by the offshore team
- Check that there is sufficient documentation for new team members
- Define clear formatting rules for any kind of documentation
- Enforce and verify code comments, annotations, and implementation notes.

3.12 Assets and Knowledge Management

Many corporations use knowledge bases for gathering reusable work products and lessons learned from past projects. Using those knowledge bases can lead to improved performance without reinventing the wheel.

Not all team members might be completely familiar with knowledge databases. In most of the studied projects, there was almost no awareness of the corporation-wide asset repository.

Recommended Approach: Promote Asset Reuse. Determine whether it is necessary to assess how reusable assets are being used and how to create new ones. Rewarding asset creation might improve motivation among practitioners to actively support and contribute to the knowledge base.

3.13 Others

During the *Global Delivery India* program, other factors emerged that can improve distributed project execution. Make sure to:

- Maintain a friendly but authoritative relationship with the offshore team
- Define responsible entities that are responsible for sub-projects
- Define an internal contract or document of understanding which includes rules that enable a smooth collaboration, and distribute it to the whole team.

4 Survey Methodology

The approach for the survey methodology is based on qualitative interviews and informal discussions. Seven projects were chosen as research cases. All projects are distributed software development projects, where the client is based in a European country and the main part of the delivery takes place in India. The types of projects are diverse, containing development and maintenance projects, as well as successful and more challenging projects.

The research data consisted of information taken from interviews of project stakeholders from both shores in Europe and India. Furthermore, different roles and positions in the project were considered. Depending on the role of the interviewee, the interviews were adapted to focus on the corresponding tasks in the project.

All information gathered from the interviewee is based on their personal experiences with globally distributed collaboration practices, which included topics such as cultural diversity, communication approach, methodology adoption, tool usage, and infrastructure set-up.

5 Conclusion and Future Work

This paper has described a set of challenges that arise on offshore projects between the European and the global delivery center shore. The recommended approaches might minimize those challenges. Although some of the suggested approaches are already in use, new questions arise: What impact does the approach have on the project? How can those approaches be integrated into the current methodologies?

Additional surveys might be conducted in future in order to answer those questions, verify the efficacy of the approaches in improving inter-shore collaboration, and to check their feasibility. There is no question that offshoring will continue, and the current economic crisis makes it more necessary than ever [17].

Acknowledgments. The *Global Delivery India* program was sponsored and supported by IBM Switzerland Global Business Services – Application Services. I would like to thank them for giving me the opportunity to go through this experience. I would also like to thank Anjali Keshava, Samuel Kurth and Bimal Mathews for their proofreading and commenting on earlier versions of this paper. Thanks to IBM India for the warm hospitality and all involved people that were always open for interviews.

References

1. Bloch, M., Jans, Ch.: Reducing risks in offshoring projects. The McKinsey Quarterly, McKinsey&Company 3 (2005),
   http://mckinseyquarterly.com/PDFDownload.aspx?ar=1634
2. Braun, A.: A Framework to Enable Offshore Outsourcing. In: International Conference on Global Software Engineering (ICGSE), pp. 125–129. IEEE, Los Alamitos (2007)
3. Carmel, E.: Global Software Teams: Collaborating Across Borders and Time Zones. Prentice Hall, Englewood Cliffs (1999)
4. Carmel, E., Agarwal, R.: The Maturation of Offshore Sourcing of Information Technology Work. In: Information Systems Outsourcing, pp. 631–650. Springer, Heidelberg (2006)
5. Christiansen, H.M.: Meeting the Challenge of Communication in Offshore Software Development. In: Meyer, B., Joseph, M. (eds.) SEAFOOD 2007. LNCS, vol. 4716, pp. 19–26. Springer, Heidelberg (2007)
6. Cristal, M., Wildt, D., Prikladnicki, R.: Usage of SCRUM Practices within a Global Company. In: International Conference on Global Software Engineering (ICGSE), pp. 222–226. IEEE, Los Alamitos (2008)
7. Hofstede, G.: Cultural Dimensions, http://www.geert-hofstede.com
8. Hofstede, G., Hofstede, G.J.: Cultures and Organizations: Software of the Mind. McGraw-Hill, New York (2005)
9. Iacono, C.S., Weisband, S.: Developing Trust in Virtual Teams. In: Proceedings of the Thirtieth Hawaii International Conference on System Sciences, pp. 412–420. IEEE, Los Alamitos (1997)
10. Itim Culture & Management Consultancy, http://www.itim.org
11. Kornstädt, A., Sauer, J.: Tackling Offshore Communication Challenges with Agile Architecture-Centric Development. In: Proceedings of the Working IEEE/IFIP Conference on Software Architecture (WICSA), pp. 44–47. IEEE, Los Alamitos (2007)

12. Matloff, N.: Offshoring: What Can Go Wrong? IT Pro., 39–45 (July-August 2005)
13. Mauch, C., Wildemann, H.: Erst analysieren, dann outsourcen. IO new management 9, 32–37 (2004)
14. Meyer, B.: Design and Code Reviews in the Age of the Internet. Communications of the ACM 51(9), 66–71 (2008)
15. Niinimäki, T., Lassenius, C.: Experiences of Instant Messaging in Global Software Development Projects: A Multiple Case Study. In: International Conference on Global Software Engineering (ICGSE), pp. 55–64. IEEE, Los Alamitos (2008)
16. Parvathanathan, K., Chakrabarti, A., Patil, P.P., Sen, S., Sharma, N., Johng, Y.: Global Development and Delivery in Practice: Experiences of the IBM Rational India Lab. IBM Redbooks (2007)
17. Spang, S.: Five trends that will shape business technology in 2009. The McKinsey Quarterly, McKinsey&Company (2009),
    http://mckinseyquarterly.com/PDFDownload.aspx?ar=2296
18. Storti, C.: Speaking of India: Bridging the Communication Gap When Working with Indians. Nicholas Brealey Publishing (2007)
19. Namaste! – IBM Schweiz beschreitet neue Wege in der Software-Entwicklung. Think! Kundenmagazin der IBM Schweiz, IBM Switzerland, May 2007, p. 5 (2007),
    http://ibm.com/ch/think/archiv/42007/pdf/IBM_Think_407_de_72.pdf

Solution Proposals for Japan-Oriented Offshore Software Development in China

Lei Zhang[1], Xuan Zhang[1], Meiping Chai[1], Yibing Tan[1],
Shigeru Miyake[1], Yoji Taniguchi[2], Jun Hosoya[2], and Ryota Mibe[2]

[1] Hitachi (China) Research & Development Corporation,
301 North Wing Tower C Raycom Infotech Park, 2 Kexueyuan Nanlu, HaidianDistrict,
Beijing, China (100190)
{leizhang,xzhang,mpchai,ybtan,smiyake}@hitachi.cn
[2] Hitachi, Ltd., Systems Development Laboratory,
Hitachi System Plaza Shinkawasaki, 890, Kashimada, Saiwai-ku, Kawasaki-shi,
Kanagawa-ken, 212-8567, Japan
{yoji.taniguchi.rf,jun.hosoya.fm,ryota.mibe.mu}@hitachi.com

Abstract. Surveys on the Japan-oriented vendors in China were conducted twice to find out the existent problems in the Japan-oriented offshore software development. From these survey results, four main problems were found out, which were the frequent requirement changes from the product owner, the misunderstanding of the requirement specification in the vendor side, the heavy overhead of the project management and the low-efficiency communication between the product owner and the vendor. Several solutions are proposed to solve these four problems, which mainly consist of the improvement of the offshore software development process and the development of the offshore development supporting tools. The proposed offshore development process is based on the application of the prototype development, the iteration development and the customer test driven development processes. The proposed offshore development supporting tools include the project management assistant tool and the communication assistant tool.

Keywords: Offshore software development, requirement change, requirement misunderstanding, project management, communication.

1 Introduction

In recent years, the offshore software development has become a popular way to decrease the software development cost and improve the core technical competence for many companies. However, some risks still exist in the offshore outsourcing, such as miscommunication, cultural difference in business customs, quality issues and so on [1][2][3]. Japan and China are two important cooperation partners in the offshore software development. However, Japanese companies also often complained that the quality was not satisfactory, and the cost turned to be much more than they expected, and so forth. [4]. It seems that the offshore software development will not definitely succeed as expected if some main issues can not be found out and solved.

O. Gotel, M. Joseph, and B. Meyer (Eds.): SEAFOOD 2009, LNBIP 35, pp. 14–24, 2009.

In order to support Japan-oriented offshore software development, many researchers in the world, especially in Japan and in China, carried out the related researches in recent years. S-open Offshoring Development Study Committee [5] conducted the surveys on the Japanese outsourcing companies and the Japan-oriented offshore vendors in China. They found out some existent problems and gave some suggestions to the offshore software development between Japan and China from the viewpoint of Japan side. Tsuji H. et al. [6] [7] presented the risk assessment scheme and tool based on the survey on many vendors in China, India or other Asian countries, in order to quantify the risk of Japanese offshore software outsourcing and promote a knowledge spiral for project management. Kojima S. and Kojima M. [8] presented some proposals for IT offshoring work for the Japanese industries based on the interviews with 21 companies, such as the strategic selection of the offshore locations, training in India and the like.

On the other hand, some researchers also conducted the studies on the general offshore software development, no relation with countries. Christiansen, H.M. [9] analyzed the factors, which have an impact on communication in the offshore software development and gave some suggestions on how to meet these challenges. Martin Fowler [10] proposed to use an agile software process in the offshore development.

Our group started the research on Japan-oriented offshore software development in China from 2005 [11] [12] [13] [14]. The surveys on Japan-oriented offshore vendors in China were conducted twice in 2006 and 2008, respectively. The main issues in Japan-oriented offshore software development in China were found out and corresponding solution proposals were presented. The proposals include the improvement of the development process and the development of the supporting tools, which will be stated in detail in the following sections.

2 Survey Results

2.1 Survey Contents

In 2006, we conducted the first survey on Japan-oriented offshore software development in China. Twenty four Japan-oriented offshore vendors were selected, most of which were ranked the top 50 vendors in China. The questionnaire included the company information, the project information, the software development process, the existent problems, the experiences and expectations. Two year later, in 2008 we carried out the second survey on Japan-oriented offshore software development in China, in order to find out whether there are new trends in this field. In this survey, 20 vendors were selected and 70% of which were selected from the 24 surveyed vendors in 2006 to make the comparison between two surveys more reasonable. The questionnaire was revised a little based on that in 2006, mainly adding some questions about the requirement change and the communication.

2.2 Existent Problems of Japan-Oriented Offshore Software Development

From the above two surveys, 10 main existent problems were found out from Japan side and China side, which are listed as follows.

Firstly, four problems were detected only from Japan side.

(1)   No special manager for one project
(2)   Too ambiguous requirement specification (RS)
(3)   Too frequent requirement changes (RC)
(4)   Low design quality
        Secondly, another four problems were discovered only from China side.
(5)   Lack of Bridge Software Engineers (BSE)
(6)   Low technology skills
(7)   Low estimation ability of delivery and cost
(8)   Many requirement misunderstanding
        Finally, two common problems were found out from both Japan and China.
(9)   Low-efficiency project management
(10) Low-efficiency communication

In our opinion, problems (1)(2)(4)(5)(6) and (7) are mainly related to the improvement of the company organization and the education level of Japan side or China side, which are difficult to be solved by the researches. While the left four problems, (3)(8)(9) and (10), may be solved to a certain extent by the improvement of the development process or the application of the supporting tools.

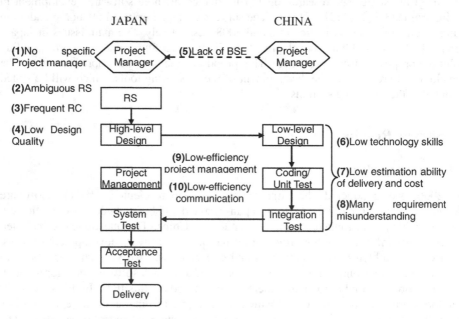

Fig. 1. Problems in Japan-oriented Offshore Software Development in China

2.3 Reasons of Main Existent Problems

Based on the survey results, the reasons of four main problems (3)(8)(9) and (10) were analyzed and summarized in Table 1. Briefly speaking, problem (3), frequent RC, was resulted from the development process of Japanese style. In such process, most requirement items generally are not fixed yet when the development is started, but becoming clear gradually with the proceeding of the development. Therefore, in this case the frequent requirement change is inevitable.

As for the problem (8) of requirement misunderstanding, one main reason is that the different culture and language between Japan and China may cause the different understanding on the same requirement item. Another main reason is that so far there is no effective way to confirm the understanding correctness of the vendor side. This means even if some requirement items are misunderstood by the vendor side, such mistake is difficult to be detected timely until these requirements are implemented and finally tested.

There are two main reasons for problem (9). First is the overhead of the project management is very big, including the data collection, the risk analysis and the report writing. Second is the skill levels of the project managers in Japan are different. Some risks can be detected timely by the experienced project managers, while may be ignored by the novices.

Table 1. Reasons of Main Existent Problems

Problem No.	Problems	Reasons
(3)	Frequent RC	· Japanese style development process (i.e. requirements are fixed gradually during the development)
(8)	Requirement misunderstanding	· Different culture and language · Lack of effective way to confirm the understanding correctness of the vendor side
(9)	Low-efficiency project management	· Overhead is very big, including data collection, risk analysis and report writing. · Risk sometimes can not be timely detected due to the poor experience of the project managers
(10)	Low-efficiency communication	· Limited communication ways (mainly E-mail and TV meeting) · Delayed feedback from the product owner · Mass and scattered information

As for the problem (10) of low-efficiency communication, the first reason is the communication ways in the offshore development is limited. Due to the cost consideration, the communication in the offshore development is mainly based on E-mail and TV meeting, which have lower efficiency compared with telephone and face to face discussion. The second reason is that in many cases, the manager in Japan is very busy every day. He/She cannot give timely feedback to the requirements from Chinese vendors. Such delayed feedback greatly affects the work efficiency of the vendor side. Furthermore, due to the limited communication ways, it is difficult to effectively remind the project manager in Japan of the reply delay. Finally, the communication contents are various in the offshore software development, such as the Q&A on the requirement or the design, the review comments on the documents, and the like. Thereby, such kind of information in the offshore development is mass and scattered.

3 Solution Proposals

In order to solve the above four main problems, we present some proposals, which are listed in Table 2. The problems of the frequent RC and the requirement misunderstanding are proposed to be solved by an improved offshore software development process, which is composed of the prototype development, the iteration development and the customer test driven development (CTDD). The problems of the low-efficiency project management and the low-efficiency communication are recommended to be resolved by the supporting tools of HOPE and FOCUS, respectively. In section 3.1-3.3, all the proposals will be stated in detail.

Table 2. Solution Proposal List for Offshore Software Development

Proposal No.	Problems to be Solved	Proposal Contents
(I)	Frequent RC	Prototype development
		Iteration development
	Requirement misunderstanding	Customer Test Driven Development (CTDD)
(II)	Low-efficiency project management	HOPE: Supporting tool of auto data collection, analysis and report generation
(III)	Low-efficiency communication	FOCUS: Supporting tool of communication acceleration and management

3.1 Proposal (I): Improved Offshore Development Process

As mentioned in Table 2, we proposed an offshore software development process, which is composed of the prototype development, the iteration development and CTDD, to improve the adaptation ability of RC and avoid the misunderstanding of RS. These three practices can be adopted in the corresponding phases of the development process shown in Fig. 2. In this figure, only the most typical work assignment between Japan side and China side are demonstrated, that is Japan side takes charge of RS, high-level design, system test and acceptance test, while China side is responsible for other left works. The application of our proposed offshore software development process generally includes the following four steps.

(i)   Japan side collects and analyzes the needs from the end-users and forms them into RS. The high-level design is also usually done by Japan side. After that the development work is transferred to China side.

(ii)   China side analyzes the change risk of the requirements and the uncertainty of the architecture approach, and then defines the scope of the prototype development, which should be agreed by Japan side. By the prototype development, China side proves the architecture and demonstrates the core requirements to Japan side. The phase of the prototype development ends after the confirmation from Japan side. Otherwise the prototype should be improved iteratively.

(iii) Other requirements will be implemented iteratively according to their priority. In iteration, firstly the iteration plan, which defines the development scope and the acceptance criteria, should be agreed by Japan side. Then China side writes the function test cases. After Japan side confirms these test cases, China side starts the low-level design, the coding, the unit test and the integration test. The confirmed function test cases will be executed in the function test phase by the end of this iteration to verify whether the implemented software meets the customer's requirements.

(iv) After Japan side completes the system test and the acceptance test, the product can be delivered finally.

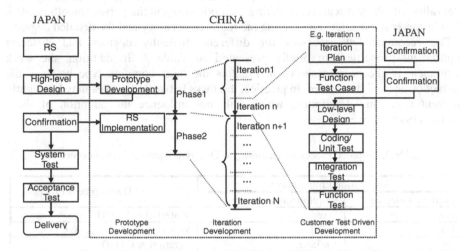

Fig. 2. Proposal of Offshore Software Development Process

Therefore, it is expected that the core requirements and the architecture can be determined as much as possible by the prototype development. This can reduce the times of the requirement change in the later phase. What's more, the fixed requirements or the requirements with higher priority are recommended to be implemented in the earlier iterations, so the ambiguous requirements can be further discussed until they become clear enough to be implemented in the later iterations. Such kind of iterative development can detect the bugs in the earlier phase and also avoid the great rework due to the requirement change in the later phase. Furthermore, if Japan side confirms the function test cases, which are written by China side, at the beginning of the iteration and China side executes the function test using these confirmed test cases at the end of this iteration, the understanding consistency of the requirements between Japan and China can be checked within iteration. This is expected to reduce the bugs which are caused by the requirement misunderstanding.

In a word, by using this improved offshore software development process, it is expected to cut down the rework cost of the requirement change, detect the bugs in the earlier stage and decrease the bugs due to the requirement misunderstanding.

Of course, the effectiveness of this process needs to be evaluated quantitatively in the real projects in the near future.

In practice, the above proposed process can be tailored according to the specific application environment, which is mainly influenced by the difficulty degree and the requirement property of a project. The difficulty degree can be judged by considering three factors: (i) Human resource, considering the business domain knowledge, the technical ability, the development experiences and the whole team cooperation ability. (ii) Reusable resource, considering the architecture, the design model and the components. (iii) Project style, considering the application software, the middleware, the embedded software, etc. The requirement property can also be decided according to three factors: (i) Requirement specification, considering its accuracy and integrality. (ii) Project scale, considering the code size and the person*month needed. (iii) Customer satisfaction, considering the required accuracy and the detailed degree.

The recommended processes for different difficulty degrees and different requirement properties are briefly presented in Table 3. In addition, the work assignment in the process shown in Fig.2 is the most common type between the product owner and the vendor. In practice, the tasks between the roles may be slightly different from this description, which will not influence the adoption of these practices essentially.

Table 3. Proposed Processes according to Different Application Environment

Application Environment		Proposed Development Process
Difficulty Degree	Requirement Property	
Easy	Fixed	Waterfall & CTDD
Hard	Fixed	Waterfall & Prototype & CTDD
Easy	Unfixed	Iteration & CTDD
Hard	Unfixed	Iteration & Prototype & CTDD

3.2 Proposal (II): Project Management Supporting Tool – HOPE

In order to cut down the overhead of the project management, some companies in Hitachi Group also considered applying some supporting tools, which can automatically collect the project data and generate the project report. However, in most cases the application of these tools will change the existent project management process to a certain extent, such as the change of the bug tracking tool, the test case sheet format and the like. Such kind of changes conversely results in the increased overhead of the project management. Therefore, the most suitable supporting tool is to automatically collect the data and generate the report, but bringing the change to the existent project management process as few as possible.

Aiming at the above targets, we developed a supporting tool named HOPE (Hitachi Offshore Project Examiner) for the offshore project management. The four main features of HOPE are shown in Fig. 3 and stated as follows.

(i)   *Good supporting of existent project management process.* In order to keep the existent project management process, all the tools (e.g. Bugzilla) or the data collection sheet (e.g. B table), which are used to collect the project data, are designed as the collector plug-ins in HOPE system. Such kind of plug-ins can be customized according to the different requirements from different companies. So the necessary project data can be collected by HOPE without changing the existent project management process in a company.

(ii)   *Automatic data collection, analysis and report generation.* HOPE automatically and periodically collects the project data from the above collector plug-ins. Furthermore, HOPE automatically analyzes these data, generates and sends the project reports to the product owner and the vendor periodically. Therefore, the overhead of the project management can be cut down.

(iii)   *Automatic rule based risk detection.* Some risk detection rules are defined in HOPE based on the experiences of the project management. By analyzing the collected data according to these rules, the project risks can be detected automatically as the exception information. Furthermore, all the rules are also design as the plug-ins in HOPE system, which can be easily customized by users. So by using HOPE, some good experiences of the project management can be easily shared within a company.

(iv)   *Different report granularities for product owner and vendor.* According to the different requirements of the product owner and the vendor, HOPE generates the report based on different data granularities. For example, the report to the product owner only includes the information of the whole project, but that to the vendor includes more detailed information, such as the information of every module.

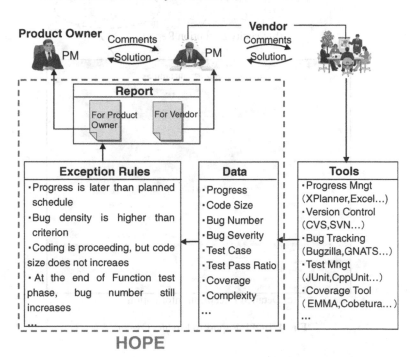

Fig. 3. Image of Offshore Project Management Tool - HOPE

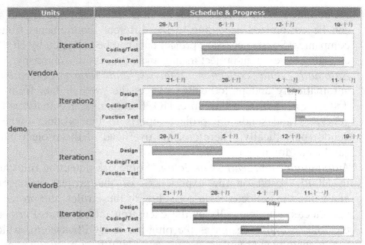

(a) Progress report

(b) Quality Exception Report

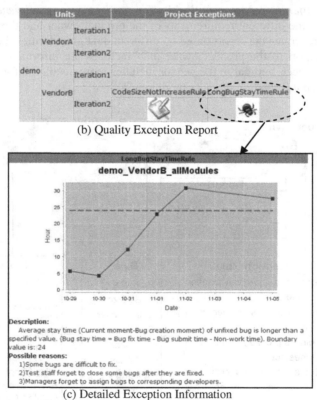

(c) Detailed Exception Information

Fig. 4. HOPE Report to Product Owner

An example of the HOPE reports to the product owner is shown in Fig.4, which consists of the progress report and the exception report. In the progress report (refer to Fig.4 (a)), the progresses for each vendor are demonstrated. If the progress is going well, the bar is shown in green color. Otherwise, the bar is shown in red color. In the quality exception report (refer to Fig.4 (b)), the detected exception information is also listed for each vendor by small icons. By clicking the icons, user can check the detailed exception information (refer to Fig.4 (c)). Herein, the related time-series data and the required criterion are shown in a chart. Also the description of the rule used for the exception detection and the possible reasons of this exception are also listed under the chart.

The format of the HOPE reports to the vendor is very similar to that to the product owner, but the data granularity is finer, such as each module's information. Furthermore, besides HTML reports, HOPE can also generate Excel reports automatically to meet the different needs of different users. So by checking the HOPE reports, the project managers in both product owner and vendor can monitor the current risks of the progress and the quality very easily and timely.

At present, HOPE is being trial used in some Hitachi associated companies. Some numerical evaluation results of HOPE will be presented after these trail uses, such as the reduction ratio of the overhead of the project management and so on.

3.3   Proposal (III): Communication and RC Supporting Tool – FOCUS

In order to solve the problem of the low-efficiency communication, we proposed a communication-supporting tool for the offshore software development, which is named FOCUS (Facilitating Offshore Communication Unified System). Because FOCUS is still under development, the detail demonstration will be omitted here. Briefly speaking, it is expected that FOCUS can cut down the overhead of the communication by the unified management of the communication content and history. Also with the periodic alert, the problem of the feedback delay can be restrained. So with FOCUS the existent problems of the communication in Japan-oriented offshore software development can be solved to a certain extent.

4   Summary

Based on the two surveys on Japan-oriented offshore vendors in China, 10 main existent problems have been found out. Except for the problems related to the company organization or the education, we present the solution proposals for four main issues, which are low-efficiency project management, low-efficiency communication, frequent requirement change and many requirement misunderstanding. The solution proposals include the improved offshore software development process and two supporting tools HOPE and FOCUS.

The improved offshore software development process is composed of the prototype, the iteration and the customer test driven development. With this process, it is expected that the adaptation ability of the requirement changes can be improved and the requirement misunderstanding can be avoided. HOPE helps the product owner and the vendor to cut down the overhead of the project management by automatic and periodic data collection and report generation, without changing the existent project management process. What's more, by the automatic rule based risk detection, the project risk can be detected timely and the good experiences of the project management can be shared easily. FOCUS is helpful for the product owner and the vendor to cut down the overhead of the communication by unified management of the communication content and history. Also the problem of the feedback delay can be solved to a certain extent.

With the above improved development process and supporting tools, some main issues in Japan-oriented offshore software development are expected to be solved. However, the effectiveness of our proposals needs evaluation in the real projects in the near future.

References

1. Aspray, W., Maydas, F., Vardi, M.Y. (eds.): Globalization and Offshoring of Software, Report of the ACM Job Migration Task Force, Association for Computing Machinery (2006)
2. Krishna, S., Sahay, S., Walsham, G.: Managing Cross-Cultural Issues in Global Software Outsourcing. CACM 47(4), 62–66 (2004)
3. Mayer, B.: The Unspoken Revolution in Software Engineering. Computer, 121–124 (January 2005)
4. Jinnai, K.: Learn from Offshoring. Project Management Magazine (in Japanese) 1, 83–103 (2005)
5. S-open Offshoring Development Study Committee: Comprehensive Guide Book on Software Development Offshoring. Nikkei BP, Tokyo (2004) (in Japanese)
6. Tsuji, H., et al.: Questionnaire-Based Risk Assessment Scheme for Japanese Offshore Software Outsourcing. In: Meyer, B., Joseph, M. (eds.) SEAFOOD 2007. LNCS, vol. 4716, pp. 114–127. Springer, Heidelberg (2007)
7. Zhongqi, S., Hiroshi, T., et al.: Preliminary Analysis for Risk Finding in Offshore Software Outsourcing from Vendor's Viewpoint. In: Second International Conference on Software Engineering Approaches For Offshore and Outsourced Development SEAFOOD, 16 pages (2008)
8. Kojima, S., Kojima, M.: Making IT Offshoring Work for the Japanese Industries. In: Meyer, B., Joseph, M. (eds.) SEAFOOD 2007. LNCS, vol. 4716, pp. 67–82. Springer, Heidelberg (2007)
9. Christiansen, H.M.: Meeting the Challenges of Communications in Offshore Software Development. In: Meyer, B., Joseph, M. (eds.) SEAFOOD 2007. LNCS, vol. 4716, pp. 19–26. Springer, Heidelberg (2007)
10. Fowler, M.: Using an Agile Software Process with Offshore Development, ThoughtWorks (2004), http://www.martinfowler.com/articles/agileOffshore.html (accessed July 26, 2004)
11. Zhang, L., Chai, M.P., Zhang, X., Miyake, S., Mibe, R.: Survey on Japan-oriented offshore software development in China. In: Meyer, B., Joseph, M. (eds.) SEAFOOD 2007. LNCS, vol. 4716, pp. 170–181. Springer, Heidelberg (2007)
12. Chai, M.P., Zhang, L., Miyake, S., Taniguchi, Y., Mibe, R.: Survey on Japan-oriented offshore software development in China. In: Proceedings of JCIS 2009, Weihai, China (2009)
13. Zhang, X., Zhang, L., Chai, M.P., Miyake, S., Mibe, R.: HOPE: Extensible system for Automatic & Periodic Diagnosis of Offshore Software Project. In: Jacko, J.A. (ed.) HCI 2007. LNCS, vol. 4553, pp. 807–815. Springer, Heidelberg (2007)
14. Zhang, L., Akifuji, S.: Comparison between Test Driven Development and Waterfall Development in a small-scale project. In: Abrahamsson, P., Marchesi, M., Succi, G. (eds.) XP 2006. LNCS, vol. 4044, pp. 211–212. Springer, Heidelberg (2006)

Working in Distributed Teams: Challenges, Best Practices, and Guidelines

Arul Mozhi Ganesan and Kayal Vizhi Ganesan

ISL, IBM India Pvt Ltd., Bangalore 560071, India
arulgane@in.ibm.com, kaganesa@in.ibm.com

Abstract. In this paper, we discuss the different challenges faced by offshore software development engineering teams – starting with the incubation period to ongoing development – from the team members' perspective. We also discuss actions taken to overcome the obstacles, and extrapolate some of the best practices and guidelines from the authors' own experience of working for more than a decade in distributed teams in multinational companies.

Keywords: Communication, cultural differences, knowledge transfer, offshore team, remote team.

1 Introduction

Many industries, including software industries, have offshore development centers in different countries all over the world. This paper discusses some of the generic challenges faced by many offshore software development engineering teams and best practices for converting the distributed team setup, consisting of teams from all over the world, into a beneficial one for business.

Section 2 focuses on the details of the following generic challenges: Challenges during ramp-up, cycle time of communication, technical expertise, schedules and festivals, communicating with the remote teams, and differences in cultural dimensions. The subsection under section 2 lists the details of each challenge, best practices to overcome the challenge, and guidelines. Section 3 provides the conclusion.

2 Challenges

The fundamental issues for distributed teams are communication, coordination, synchronization due to time zone differences, and cultural differences. This paper discusses challenges faced by distributed team members and describes how the challenges can be addressed.

In this paper, the keywords counterpart team or remote team refer to the onsite software engineering team with whom the offshore software development engineering team needs to interact or work.

O. Gotel, M. Joseph, and B. Meyer (Eds.): SEAFOOD 2009, LNBIP 35, pp. 25–31, 2009.

2.1 Challenges during Ramp-Up

Challenge 1
Most often the offshore software development teams are started as an extended team of the existing development teams in the United States, the United Kingdom, or Canada. The new offshore engineering teams are not provided with complete details about their counterparts in the existing teams.

During initial setup, very few knowledge transfer sessions from the existing team are given with focus on the technical details of the projects to be executed. Most of the time, information regarding setting up the work environment, access to the systems, and access to the lab machines in the remote team is not provided formally. This information may not be formally documented. Usually the information is obtained when discussing with various team members from counterpart teams through email/phone or on need basis. Due to the formal non-availability of basic information, there is a delay or there is an increase in the ramp up time. To overcome these initial hurdles, the following tips could be practiced.

Best Practices 1
1. When knowledge transfer is provided by the counterpart teams, record those sessions with audio and demos given. Use tools such as IBM Lotus Sametime® and other web meeting tools that have recording options, options to replay and convert into different formats. It is very useful for the team members to refer and play back for better understanding.
2. Capture all the information gathered in a document.
   a.   Details of the team members in the counterpart team:
      1.   Their roles and responsibilities
      2.   Their tasks on the team
      3.   Their technical areas of expertise
      4.   Contact details, such as email address and phone numbers
      5.   Preferred mode of communication (either email, phone, or chat)
      6.   Preferred time to contact
   b.   Details of the various development and execution systems available in the counterpart team (most of the time, the offshore development teams may not have the complete lab setup, and might need access to the setups from remote teams)
   c.   Procedure or permissions to get access rights to the development and lab systems or machines, including details of the contact person (or tool), to create user names and passwords in the remote environment
   d.   Details of the source code version control tools used by the remote teams, the configuration procedure to create a workspace, and the location or repository details of the workspaces
   e.   Details of the compilation environment and procedures to execute and debug
   Convert the information into a PDF format and name the document *Newbie Guide*. When a new member joins the team, he/she can refer to the *Newbie Guide* and then can more easily prepare for working with the team

3. Create a central database (or team room database) and keep all the required documents so that they can be easily accessed through a web link. It serves as a central repository of documents and all the project related documents are easily available in one place.

These best practices can help the offshore team members to speed up and reduce the initial ramp-up time.

Guidelines 1

- Recording the knowledge transfer sessions to create a useful resource for replaying later.
- Maintain a simple document capturing details of the team members, work environment setups, and details for getting access to the lab environments.
- Keep all the documents and references in a wiki page, Web link, or database that can be accessed by all the team members.

2.2 Cycle Time of Communication

Challenge 2

In an extended team setup, few modules of the entire project/product are handled by the offshore software development teams. The rest of the modules are handled by counterpart team members from different geographies.

For technical problems or issues related to the project, the offshore team members often send a mail to the counterpart team by the end of their business day. Many times there is no overlapping of working hours between offshore development teams and counterpart teams. Hence, the responses are received by the next business day.

To resolve a problem, sometimes, a couple of days of email exchanges between the offshore teams and counterpart teams occur. These kinds of communication styles tend to increase the cycle time to find the resolution for the problem.

The following best practices can be used to reduce the cycle time to resolve issues.

Best Practices 2

1. It is observed from working in the software industry that some of the offshore software development team members, and also the counterpart team members, work at a time that is convenient for them. When you need a clarification from the distributed team member from a different geographic location, don't wait to send the email at the end of your business day. Instead, whenever in doubt, send out the email immediately. Sometimes, the respective counterpart/concerned team member might be working late or early, and will have the opportunity to respond immediately.
2. Another option is to send an email to determine a convenient time to talk over chat or telephone and get clarification, which significantly reduces the total time taken to resolve the issue.
3. Do not forget to document or record the details of clarifications provided or technical assistance provided by the remote team in the team room database. This information could be useful for other team members with similar questions.

Guidelines 2
Working in a distributed team, whenever you need a clarification from the remote team:

- Send out the mail immediately. Don't wait for the end of the business day to send the mail.
- When possible, either chat with them or have a meeting.
- Record the information for later reference.

2.3   Technical Expertise

Challenge 3
Most often, when the offshore software development teams are working as an extended team from different geographic location, complete project details and expertise are not available. Information for only a few of the modules of the entire project is available in offshore development teams.

When an obstacle or technical problem happens, the offshore development team might need to wait to receive clarification from their counterparts. There can be confusion and arguments regarding the root cause of the problem, as the complete knowledge of the product/project or expertise are not available.

Best Practices 3
Technical expertise should be built locally, either by assigning a dedicated technical lead for the team or by pooling some of the senior engineers or technical managers from different groups. These technical experts should have expertise and technical skills in specific domains. They should be trained to have the knowledge of the entire project/product, debugging skills, and the ability to analyze issues reported from customers. They should be able to guide and resolve day to day technical issues such as domain specific queries, debugging, core file analysis, and so on.

Whenever there are technical issues, the local technical experts should be contacted first. The local technical experts should be able to provide initial guidance for analyzing the problem and to find out the root cause. If absolutely necessary, and if the problem cannot be solved locally by the offshore development team, then the remote team needs to be contacted for further assistance.

Building local technical expertise significantly improves the problem resolution time, and also provides more commitment and involvement and sense of ownership from the offshore development teams.

Guidelines 3
- Build local team technical expertise in the offshore development team, with technical skills on a specific domain. This expertise can be leveraged for initial problem analysis and resolution.

2.4   Schedules and Local Festivals

Challenge 4
Most of the time, the project schedules are driven from the remote teams, without taking into account of the local holidays and festivals in the offshore development

team, For example, in India, festivals such as Diwali and Dashara are important celebrations, and most people plan their vacation with their families during these times.

If projects are scheduled to be delivered during the local festival time of the offshore development team, there might be some unnecessary delay in the project due to key resources or team members taking their vacation. It is difficult to ask employees not to take leave during the festival to accommodate project release dates; it might demoralize the team members of the offshore development teams.

Best Practices 4
1. Project schedules and deliverables need to be finalized after discussion with the offshore development team. This approach will boost the offshore development team's confidence and satisfaction level, as due respect is given to their culture and values. Also, the offshore development teams should communicate their vacation timing well in advance, during the time of planning itself.
2. On the other hand, many counterpart teams from the United States, the United Kingdom or Canada plan their leave or long weekends, holidays, or vacations during the months of December and January. Both the offshore and remote teams could formally discuss and schedule the offshore team members as backup, which will increase the high availability of the product or project handled by the teams to the customer. In some cases where this arrangement is not possible, the offshore team can also plan for their own team development activities during this time.
3. In general, mark the holidays of both teams in the calendar/schedule. Having done that, the teams will know the availability of the other team members when scheduling meetings and can schedule the project deadlines based on that. Tools like IBM Lotus Notes® have options to remind individuals of the upcoming holidays marked in their calendar.

Guidelines 4
- Communicate your holidays and vacations well in advance to the counterpart team.
- Mark the calendar with the counterpart team's official holidays.
- When scheduling the project release and target dates, considers both offshore and remote teams' holiday seasons.

2.5 Communicating with the Remote Team

Challenge 5
Most often, offshore team members tend to speak fast, unlike the Americans/British who are the native English speakers. They tend to use abbreviations, jargons, and acronyms (which are mostly common only in the native counties) in a conference call, while interacting with the remote team.

Best Practices 5
To avoid communication hurdles, the following tips can be used.

1. Nowadays, most companies have an intranet text messaging service (text chat). Invite all the participants to a text chat, while starting the voice-based conference

call. If anyone in the conference call has difficultly in understanding another person, or any particular sentence or word, they can ask the person to type in the chat window.
2. Always speak slowly while communicating with the remote team.
3. Summarize the meeting details and make sure everyone understands
4. Always send minutes of the meeting immediately after a voice conference call with the remote team.

By following these tips, everyone will have the same understanding with better clarity, and it will be easier to follow up on action items.

Guidelines 5
If possible, use a text-based messaging system along with a voice based one for better understanding and clarity in communication.

2.6 Differences in Cultural Dimensions

Challenge 6
In a distributed team setup, it is possible to have teams that are culturally very different. A few of the differences are

1. In offshore teams, there are large gaps between levels of the organization. They always provide group opinions rather than individual opinions, and they talk more about the group's need, unlike their counterparts from western countries (United States/United Kingdom/Canada, etc.), where there are fewer gaps between managers and subordinates and each are expected to have their own opinions and concerns.
2. In general, offshore team members tend to over commit. Rather than being very straightforward and not hesitating to say "No" They think more about the future and long-term aspects, unlike western counterparts who focus very much on the task at hand.

Best Practices 6
A few tips to achieve success factors are:

1. Set realistic objectives and time frames
2. Understand the orientation of other cultures and their potential impacts
3. Familiarize yourself with your counterpart's cultures, customs, and traditions
4. Focus on relating to individuals rather than thinking in terms of cultural stereotypes
5. Focus on creating value out of differences rather than trying to assimilate or avoid the differences
6. Recognize that there is tremendous potential for breakthroughs in having a problem solved in a new way.

Guidelines 6
- Recognize that there are differences and prepare for them.
- Adapt behaviors to make working together easier and more successful.
- Help others work effectively across cultures.

3 Conclusion

Having teams distributed geographically has advantages and business benefits. The teams internally face many challenges due to time zone differences, cultural differences, communication gaps, and environmental differences. The guidelines given in this paper will help them to overcome a few of those issues. The benefits we gain from distributed teams are plusses and the issues are many. Hence, it is important to address the challenges or difficulties as early as possible and to understand each other to get the best results from the distributed team.

Disclaimer: The work presented is that of the authors and IBM® is not responsible or liable for any information presented in this paper.

References

1. Hofstede, G.: Culture's Consequences: International Differences in Work-Related Values. Sage Publications, Newbury Park (1984)
2. Culture Clash Quick Cases, http://w3-03.ibm.com/manager/simulations/simi5.nsf/Pages/HomePage

Quantitative CMMI Assessment for Offshoring through the Analysis of Project Management Repositories

Thanwadee Sunetnanta[1], Ni-On Nobprapai[1], and Olly Gotel[2]

[1] Mahidol University, Department of Computer Science, Bangkok, Thailand
cctth@mahidol.ac.th, g4637267@student.mahidol.ac.th
[2] Pace University, Department of Computer Science, New York, NY, USA
ogotel@pace.edu

Abstract. The nature of distributed teams and the existence of multiple sites in offshore software development projects pose a challenging setting for software process improvement. Often, the improvement and appraisal of software processes is achieved through a turnkey solution where best practices are imposed or transferred from a company's headquarters to its offshore units. In so doing, successful project health checks and monitoring for quality on software processes requires strong project management skills, well-built onshore-offshore coordination, and often needs regular onsite visits by software process improvement consultants from the headquarters' team. This paper focuses on software process improvement as guided by the Capability Maturity Model Integration (CMMI) and proposes a model to evaluate the status of such improvement efforts in the context of distributed multi-site projects without some of this overhead. The paper discusses the application of quantitative CMMI assessment through the collection and analysis of project data gathered directly from project repositories to facilitate CMMI implementation and reduce the cost of such implementation for offshore-outsourced software development projects. We exemplify this approach to quantitative CMMI assessment through the analysis of project management data and discuss the future directions of this work in progress.

Keywords: CMMI appraisal, CMMI assessment, offshore software development, project management, quantitative analysis, SCAMPI, software process improvement.

1 Introduction and Motivation

Software process improvement (SPI) is often promoted to ensure more disciplined project management, better project control and (ultimately) enhanced quality in software development products. In practice, SPI efforts are commonly guided and appraised through process improvement approaches such as the Capability Maturity Model Integration (CMMI), as governed by the Software Engineering Institute (SEI) [1]. In the particular context of offshore software development, there can be a strong need to attain a CMMI quality rating at a particular maturity level as it is perceived as

O. Gotel, M. Joseph, and B. Meyer (Eds.): SEAFOOD 2009, LNBIP 35, pp. 32–44, 2009.

an important factor that contributes to the likely success of the work delivered. Such maturity level ratings further play a very important role in defining how the software development process will be structured and applied to each offshore development unit [2]. From the view of offshore business centers or suppliers, appraisal at a certain CMMI maturity level can maximize their chances of winning business from companies that are pursuing offshore outsourcing services. From the view of onshore business centers or headquarters, working with offshore partners who have gained an appraisal at a requisite CMMI maturity level can help them minimize risk in their outsourced projects.

A quick path to CMMI adoption and implementation in offshore settings can be to impose or transfer a turnkey solution and the best practices from an onshore headquarters to its offshore units. This is often done by providing the offshore units with a collection of procedures, checklists, templates and standards to which the offshore units must conform in their development processes. In so doing, successful project health checks and monitoring for sustained quality on software processes requires strong project management skills, well-built onshore-offshore coordination and regular onsite visits by the SPI consultants from the headquarters' team. A case study has demonstrated the importance of such knowledge transfer from multinational corporations to their subsidiaries so as to build up a knowledge base, improve capabilities, accelerate management localization, and survive intense competition, thereby generating good returns for their parent companies [3]. However, the nature of distributed software development teams and the existence of multiple sites in offshore software development arrangements still pose a challenging setting in which to perform all the necessary management, coordination and consultation tasks.

Though the benefits of attaining a high CMMI maturity level rating are obvious, CMMI adoption and implementation can be costly, time-consuming and complex, especially for low-cost development countries which are the emerging markets for IT and business process offshoring. It is clearly stated by the SEI that the CMMI is a model, not a process standard [4]. The CMMI suggests what to do and what work products should be produced to achieve process quality, but it does not say how to do the process and its essential activities. When systems software engineering is outsourced, providing guidance on how to interpret the CMMI is desirable [5]. Therefore, one factor in successful CMMI interpretation and implementation for offshoring contexts is to overcome any cross-border culture and language barriers in the transition of CMMI practices. Fast-growing offshore outsourcing software development industries in countries like India and those in Central and Eastern Europe may be able to adopt CMMI without the barriers or with fewer barriers of language and culture. However, for other offshoring countries like China, three major obstacles to CMM/CMMI implementation have been reported. The obstacles are over-complex and dogmatic CMMI implementation processes (65%), the high cost of the implementation (52%) and other issues such as the lack of automated supporting tools (<5 %) [6].

This paper proposes to apply a model of *quantitative* CMMI assessment for the benefit of SPI in offshore software development projects to address some of these obstacles. We use the term CMMI 'assessment' to emphasize the fact that what we propose in this paper does not intend to replace a full and traditional CMMI appraisal (as outlined in Section 2). Rather, it seeks to provide complementary and supporting evidence of process quality and improvement, in an ongoing continual assessment basis and with less need for site visits. Note that this would not eliminate the need for site visits and personnel interviews to gather evidence, but it could help to prepare for such appraisal activities more pointedly. By 'quantitative', we mean that the assessment results are calculated from objective evidence that is collected by way of data gathered during the regular course of project development. This is in contrast to traditional CMMI appraisals where project evidence is collected at the time of appraisal, so often in a post-hoc manner.

Tools to support traditional appraisals tend to provide web-based forms or templates to collect project evidence when an appraisal in underway. Such tools typically act more like assistants, providing a navigable structure to help the appraisers gather suitable evidence, a mechanism to record, collate and manage the evidence, and graphical techniques to present the data and resulting maturity profiles for analysis purposes. Example tools include the Interim Maturity Toolkit [9] and CMMiPal [10]. The Interim Maturity Toolkit provides users with spreadsheets to fill in a score from 0 to 10 representing the frequency with which each CMMI practice is conducted, a "?" for 'I don't know', or a "m" for 'this is not applicable'. CMMiPal uses a database to record objective appraisal evidence. If the evidence is provided for a CMMI practice, then CMMiPal indicates that the practice is done. Other example tools include the Appraisal Assistant (free and general purpose) [7] and the CMMI Appraisal Recorder (commercial) [8]. Given that tool functionality is quite straightforward and similar, many appraisers commonly develop their own proprietary tools to support their tasks. While the results of existing CMMI appraisal tools are generalized in the form of "Do" and "Not-Do" options, our work attempts to classify objective assessment evidence, retrieve this evidence from project repositories, count this evidence, and construct statistical models in an attempt to explain what is observed.

When objective evidence about a project's activity is collectively stored in a repository for quantification, it allows tasks for local CMMI implementation at an offshore site to be monitored remotely by its headquarters or onshore center. Well-built offshore coordination for CMMI assessment is therefore implicitly achieved through this quantitative CMMI assessment model, thereby reducing the demands of monitoring tasks and the onsite visits associated with CMMI implementation in such settings. Although our first intention in developing this quantitative assessment model was to provide measurable and indicative CMMI assessment results, so as to gauge process quality and guide improvement activities, we also suggest that such a quantitative approach would ease the process of planning and preparing for a fuller appraisal, as well as offer supporting evidence for the appraisal itself.

In Section 2, we describe our quantitative CMMI assessment model and illustrate how it is applied to offshore software development. Section 3 then shows the details of our quantitative CMMI assessment process and rules. We illustrate this approach to quantitative CMMI assessment through the analysis of a project management repository in Section 4, and finish with conclusions and a summary of ongoing work in Section 5.

2 Quantitative CMMI Assessment Model for Offshoring

Our assumption is that the objective evidence for quantitative CMMI assessment can be automatically gathered and measured from an analysis of the existence of key project configuration items (CIs), such as work breakdown structures, requirement reviews, test documents, etc., held in project repositories. While software developers at an offshore site work, the project CIs that are constructed or delivered as part of the development process can be collected into a local project CI repository. Our quantitative CMMI assessment process then makes use of the data in this repository for local CMMI assessment. Considering that a project may be split and outsourced to different offshore units, the local project CI repositories of different offshore sites can be pooled together into an integrated project CI repository for global quantitative CMMI assessment to monitor the quality of the development process as a whole. Fig. 1 depicts this quantitative CMMI assessment concept in a distributed offshore setting.

To conduct the analysis of project CIs for quantitative CMMI assessment, a CMMI appraiser is required to set up rules to identify which project CIs will be suitable as objective evidence of the different sub-practices of the CMMI. This rule setting activity is done as a pre-process to the assessment. To define the same assessment standard for every offshore unit of a single company, a set of assessment rules can be set once and then applied to all the units. Fig. 2 summarizes the main use cases and actors in our assessment model.

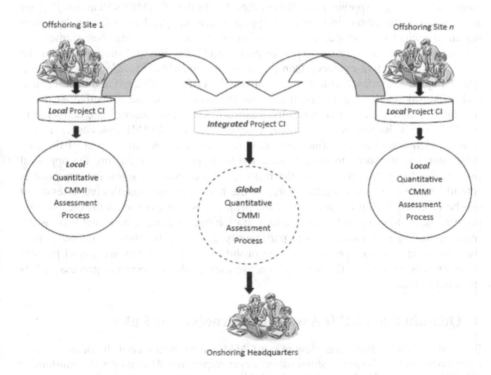

Fig. 1. Overview of Quantitative CMMI Assessment for Offshoring

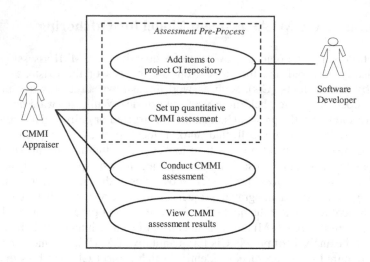

Fig. 2. Use Cases, Actors and Associations in the Quantitative CMMI Assessment Model

The model of our quantitative CMMI assessment aligns with the phases of SCAMPI, the Standard CMMI Appraisal Method for Process Improvement, as designed by the SEI [11]. The SCAMPI phases consist of Plan and Prepare for Appraisal, Conduct Appraisal and Report Results. In the SCAMPI's Plan and Prepare for Appraisal phase, requirements for appraisal are analyzed in order to determine appraisal objectives, scope, constraints, outputs, and to obtain commitment to appraisal input. Following the appraisal plan, team selection and preparation for the collection of objective evidence then proceeds. In the SCAMPI's Conduct Appraisal phase, objective evidence will then be examined, verified, validated and documented, and appraisal results are determined from the analysis of the objective evidence presented. Finally, the appraisal results, lessons learned and feedback are delivered in the SCAMPI's Report Results phase. Our quantitative CMMI assessment model follows such activities as defined by SCAMPI. However, we move part of the data collection activity so as to collect some evidence prior to conducting the appraisal proper. By doing this, we reduce the tasks and time required when the appraisal is actually being conducted. Furthermore, as the results of our quantitative assessment can be calculated from the analysis of the project CIs that exist at any stage during a project, the monitoring of CMMI implementation can be done in near real-time as the implementation progresses. This is particularly appealing for those situations where the cost of an external appraisal may be prohibitive but where awareness of process maturity is beneficial. In the next section, we explain this assessment process and its rules in more detail.

3   Quantitative CMMI Assessment Process and Rules

Fig. 3 shows the architectural view of our CMMI assessment model. It consists of two main components: *Project Configuration Items Repository Manager* and *Quantitative CMMI Assessment Engine*. A dotted border box in the figure indicates the boundary of each component.

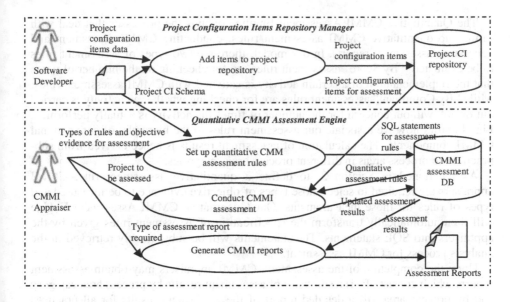

Fig. 3. Architectural View of Quantitative CMMI Assessment

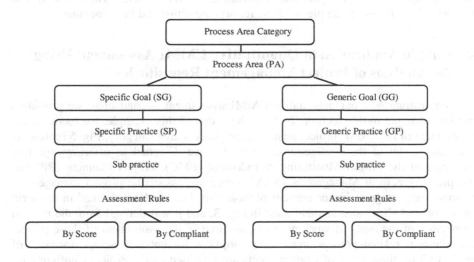

Fig. 4. Hierarchy of Conventional CMMI Components and Associated Assessment Rules

Software developers use the Project Configuration Items Repository Manager to add details of project configuration items as the project development progresses. In our implementation, we design project CI schema representing the data model of configuration items to be collected. An example of the data model is shown in the next section. Details of the project CI will be retained in the project CI repository to be retrieved for further analysis and CMMI assessment.

The Quantitative CMMI Assessment Engine contains the processes that deal with setting up quantitative CMMI assessment rules, conducting CMMI assessment and generating assessment reports. In our model, there are two types of assessment rules to be evaluated: "By Score" assessment rules are for checking on the number of times that the implementation of a certain activity is satisfied with CMMI assessment rules; while "By Compliant" assessment rules are for checking whether an activity is carried out or not, without concern for the number of times the activity is actually performed. Fig. 4 shows how we associate our assessment rules to the hierarchy of conventional CMMI components. The calculation of assessment results is hence derived from sub-practices to process areas in different process area categories.

As mentioned in Section 2, to define a quantitative assessment rule, CMMI appraisers are required to select those types of objective evidence to be measured and types of rules for those measurements. Our Quantitative CMMI Assessment Engine will then automatically transform the specification of assessment rules given by the appraisers into SQL statements. The statements will be subsequently retrieved in the analysis process for CMMI assessment.

Upon the completion of the assessment, CMMI appraisers may obtain assessment reports which consist of: (i) a summary of assessment results by process area category and by process area; (ii) a detailed report of the assessment results for all practices and sub-practices; and (iii) an assessment report in the form of an area chart diagram showing the relative strengths and weaknesses of the Specific Goals (SGs) and Generic Goals (GGs). Examples of these reports are illustrated in the next section.

4   Sample Application of Quantitative CMMI Assessment Using the Analysis of Project Management Repositories

To demonstrate how our quantitative CMMI assessment is conducted, we provide a worked example in this section. To limit the scope of this example, we focus on the assessment of the CMMI project management process area category. Fig. 5 represents the data model of the configuration items that we designed as offering objective evidence of the Project Monitoring and Control (PMC), Project Planning (PP) and Supplier Agreement Management (SAM) process areas of the project management process area category. In our implementation, this data model is defined in the form of the project CI schema as mentioned in Fig. 3, and it was derived from the manual inspection of the types of work products required in the assessment of these project management related process areas. The templates for entering actual instances of project CI for these types of work products are provided by the Project Configuration Items Repository Manager, which was described in the previous section. The instances explain relevant attributes of project configuration items. For example, a *project* instance is defined with the attributes of project ID, organization ID, customer ID, project name, project description, project objective, project manager, overall budget and actual cost. Likewise, a work breakdown structure or WBS instance is defined with its ID and details of tasks that are contained in the structure, including task name, task description, task category and phases. The attribute values of an instance will be checked for the quantified results of an assessment as specified by predefined assessment rules.

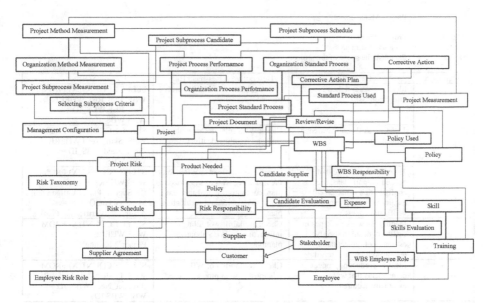

Fig. 5. Logical Data Model of Project CI Repository of Project Management Related Process Areas

Fig. 6 exemplifies some of the rules that have been defined for this example. The description of tasks required for the sub-practices was obtained from the CMMI standard. The assessment rules defined in the figure are samples of the selection of objective evidence by CMMI appraisers for each of the sub-practices. The research methodology for defining the rules is to firstly inspect the assessment requirements specified by CMMI sub-practices, then to select the relevant objective evidence from the project CI repository, and then finally to determine whether the assessment of the sub-practices should be done by score or by compliance as previously defined in Section 3. The SQL statements shown in Fig. 6 are quantitative CMMI rules that were automatically generated by our Quantitative CMMI Assessment Engine in response to the selection of objective evidence and assessment requirements. Note that the specification of quantitative assessment rules can be made at a fine-grained level to define criteria on the attributes of project configuration items. An example can be seen from the grey highlighted rule of sub-practice 1 of SP 1.1 of SG 1 in the Project Planning Practice Area in Fig. 6.

To demonstrate how the Quantitative CMMI Assessment Engine will generate the results of a quantitative CMMI assessment from the analysis of project management repositories, assume that we are conducting a CMMI assessment for the ABC Company whose nature of business is software services and solutions. The ABC Company has outsourced its inventory system development to an offshore unit. The offshore unit maintains records of how they have dealt with suppliers and managed product needs, but they rarely documented details on project tasks.

Category   Project Management

PA: Project Planning
SG 1:   Establish Estimate
SP 1.1   Establish the scope of the project

Subpractice	Description	Descriptive Assessment Rule	SQL
1	Identify risks and their mitigation tasks	Check relationship of WBS with project risk	SELECT COUNT(X) FROM WBS, Proj_Risk WHERE (Proj_Risk.WBS_ID = WBS.WBS_ID)
	Tasks for skill and knowledge acquisition	Check WBS relationship with skill and training identified	SELECT COUNT(X) FROM WBS, Skill_Need WHERE (Skill_Need.WBS_ID = WBS.WBS_ID)
	Tasks for development of needed support plans, such as configuration management, quality assurance, and verification plans	Check tasks defined in WBS for the task categories of supported plan, configuration management, quality assurance and verification plan	SELECT COUNT(X) FROM WBS WHERE Task_Category IN (Support Plan, Configuration Management, Quality Assurance, Verification Plan)
2	Identify the work packages in sufficient detail to specify estimates of project tasks, responsibilities, and schedule	Check availability of filling information in WBS about planning	SELECT COUNT(X) FROM WBS WHERE Phase="Planning"
3	Identify product or product components that will be externally acquired	Check availability of WBS relationship with product needed	SELECT COUNT(X) FROM WBS, Product_Need WHERE (Product_Need.WBS_ID = WBS.WBS.ID)
4	Identify work products that will be reused	Check availability of reused material in WBS	SELECT COUNT(X) FROM WBS WHERE Reused_Material IS NOT NULL

SP 1.2   Establish estimate of work product and task attributes

Subpractice	Description	Descriptive Assessment Rule	SQL
1	Determine the technical approach for the project	Check availability of project document with document type of technical approach document	SELECT COUNT(X) FROM WBS, Proj_Doc WHERE WBS.WBS_ID = Proj_Doc.WBS_ID AND Proj_Doc.Doc_Type = "Technical Approach"
2	Use appropriate methods to determine the attributes of the work products and tasks that will be used to estimate the resource requirements	Check availability of WBS relationship with project measurement	SELECT COUNT(X) FROM WBS, Proj_Measurement WHERE (Proj_Measurement.WBS_ID = WBS.WBS_ID)
3	Estimate the attributes of the work products and tasks	Count ratio of expected work product in WBS table	SELECT COUNT(X) FROM WBS WHERE Expected_WP IS NOT NULL; SELECT COUNT(X) FROM WBS;

SP 1.3   Define project life cycle

Subpractice	Description	Descriptive Assessment Rule	SQL
1	Define the project lifecycle phases on which to scope the planning effort	Check availability of phase in WBS table	SELECT COUNT(X) FROM WBS WHERE Phase IS NOT NULL

Fig. 6. Sample Quantitative Assessment Rules for the Project Management Process Area Category

Fig. 7 shows the existence (or not) of project configuration items in the project management repository of the ABC Company's offshore unit. For this sample case, there are some configuration items or work products that the ABC Company produces

CI Types	Project Scheduling	Risk Management	Resource Management	Document Management	Skill and Training Management	Supplier Agreement Management	Stakeholder Management
Existence	Some	None	None	None	None	Some	None

Fig. 7. Status of Project Configuration Items for ABC Company's Offshore Unit

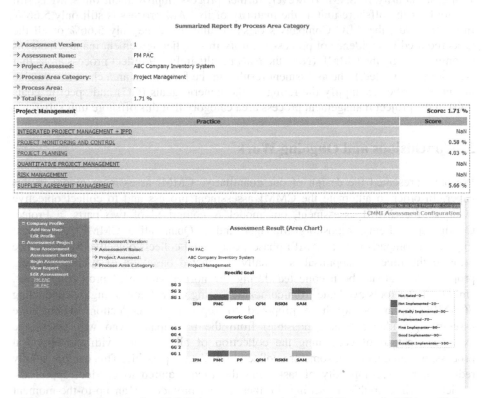

Fig. 8. Sample Quantitative CMMI Assessment Result for ABC Company's Offshore Unit

that provide evidence of project schedule planning and supplier agreement management activities. Nonetheless, the company does not hold evidence that they conduct any activities related to managing risk, resources, documents, skills, training and stakeholders. In other words, the project configuration items related to those activities do not exist in the ABC Company's project management data repository.

Fig. 8 illustrates the assessment results that can be obtained from this example. The numbers that are the results of this assessment for each practice are calculated from the assessment rules that were generated for quantifying the project CI in the project management repository. The existence of CI types for project scheduling and supplier agreement management results in the assessment scores in the areas of Project Monitoring and Control, Project Planning, and Supplier Agreement Management.

From Fig. 8, we can see the assessment results that indicate not only whether the practices are done in the areas but also the numbers representing the percentage of project configuration items that match the objective evidence as defined for the assessment of each practice or process area. It can also be seen that the overall maturity of the project management process area of the offshore unit of the ABC Company is very low (1.71%). Out of PMC, PP and SAM, this offshore unit has the strongest maturity in SAM. However, further process improvement on SAM is still required for the offshore unit as the maturity of its SAM process is still only 5.66%. In other words, the ABC Company's offshore unit has done only 5.66% of all the tasks required for evidence of process maturity in supplier agreement management, as recommended by the CMMI. (Note the NaN results in Fig. 9 reflect process areas that are not yet supported.) The assessment results, in the form of an area chart shown also in Fig. 9, further exemplify the rating of the generic goals (GG) and specific goals (SG) in the project management process area category that this offshore unit satisfies.

5   Conclusions and Ongoing Work

We have presented the design of our quantitative CMMI assessment model in this paper. In order to automate the CMMI assessment process and to collect objective evidence for CMMI assessment, our model is comprised of two parts: a Project Configuration Items Repository Manager and a Quantitative CMMI Assessment Engine. In comparison to SCAMPI phases, our model collects objective SPI evidence prior to the time the appraisal is actually conducted based on examining existing project data that has been collected during the normal course of project activities. Unlike similar tools available from companies doing CMMI consulting or conducting SCAMPI appraisals, we have proposed to separate the collection of objective assessment evidence (where possible) from the participants who will assess the evidence. Instead of combining the collection of all evidence with the appraisal process, we anticipate that some pre-collection of data is possible. This can potentially reduce both the complexity of tasks and the time required to conduct appraisals, particularly in a multi-site setting. Further, it can provide for an up-to-the-moment perspective on both local and integrated levels in such settings.

To evaluate our model, we have developed a CMMI assessment tool and have designed the assessment rules for the Project Monitoring and Control (PMC), Project Planning (PP) and Supplier Agreement Management (SAM) project management process areas of the CMMI. We used VB.NET to implement the Project Configuration Items Repository Manager for the data entry of the project configuration items and we used ASP.NET to implement a web-based application for the CMMI assessment, which is equipped with our Quantitative CMMI Assessment Engine. The tool was exercised with test cases to provide for a preliminary inspection of the correctness of the assessment rules in the form of the SQL statements that were automatically generated by our Quantitative CMMI Assessment Engine, as well as to evaluate the correctness of the assessment results as measured from the analysis of the project management data of the test cases. To fully test our model for quantitative CMMI assessment, more work needs to be done to define additional rules for the remaining process areas in the project management process area category, such as Integrated

Project Management, Quantitative Project Management and Risk Management. We are currently investigating how to import the project management data from existing project management tools so that the assessment can be done based on the content of project configuration items held in such tools directly, thus easing the process. Future work also involves extending the design of the project's CI repository and its data entry to include additional CIs from other software development phases beyond project management. Although it may require intensive expert experience and human work at the onset to set up the assessment rules, the set up is required once and passed on to multiple offshoring sites where the similar practice of CMMI assessment is required. As with the appraisal process in general, where the selection of appropriate evidence depends upon the skill and integrity of the appraiser, the assessment rules are likewise pivotal. However, ensuring the quality and consistency of the SEI's process appraisal technology is outside the scope of our current work.

Although in its early stages, this work has begun to demonstrate how quantitative CMMI assessment can be achieved through the analysis of project configuration items that can be collected automatically, remotely and cumulatively while a software development project is in progress, irrespective of the global distribution of project units and without the need for software developers to change their everyday practices to explicitly enable such continual assessment. In so doing, we suggest that it will help to reduce the cost and effort of SPI implementation for offshore software development, especially in emerging offshoring countries where the costs of such programs are prohibitive and the guidelines are not so well established. The quantitative assessment results generated from our model are primarily intended to form part of an internal or self-appraisal program, so facilitating and guiding CMMI interpretation and implementation. In this way, our model can be considered as a complementary technique to the wider appraisal activities that are demanded by SCAMPI, not a replacement. However, the benefit is that it does offer precise measurement and analysis of objective assessment evidence by explicit programming queries and statistical models instead of relying solely on an individuals' interpretation of the existence of objective assessment evidence.

Further work is required to put this work into practice with real project data and to evaluate its practicality and appeal to the wider software industry. Its role in supporting SPI in offshoring contexts will be the primary target of our studies. At this current stage of the work, we have demonstrated that the assessment rules proposed in this model can enable the quantified measurement and quality rating of process activities or work products relative to CMMI criteria. The validation of this model, process and supporting tool by CMMI appraisers, and the usefulness of the outputs generated, will need to be further investigated as the next step. The quality of the rules set for CMMI assessment in this model will be validated further, by inspecting the precision and recall of the outputs returned by the rules in comparison to the outputs of manual CMMI assessment. Time factors, such as the time required in setting the rules and analyzing the outputs, in comparison to the time required for manual assessment, will also be studied to examine the time saving that use of this tool may bring. We plan to make the tool freely available for others to use so as to enable this next validation step.

References

1. Software Engineering Institute (SEI): CMMI for Development Version 1.2. Carnegie Mellon University, Pittsburgh (2006)
2. Pilatti, L., Audy, J.L.N.: Global Software Development Offshore Insourcing Organizations Characteristics Lessons Learned from a Case Study. In: IEEE International Conference on Global Software Engineering (ICGSE 2006) (2006)
3. Wanga, P., Tongb, T.W., Koh, C.P.: An Integrated Model of Knowledge Transfer from MNC Parent to China subsidiary. Journal of World Business 39, 168–182 (2004)
4. Software Engineering Institute (SEI), CMMI? Or Agile: Why Not Embrace Both!, http://www.sei.cmu.edu/pub/documents/08.reports/08tn003.pdf
5. Konrad, M., Chrissis, M.B., Curtis, B., Paulk, M.: A Report on the May 2002 CMMI® Workshop, Adoption Barriers and Benefits for Commercial Software and Information Systems Organizations, Software Engineering Institute (2002), http://www.sei.cmu.edu/pub/documents/02.reports/pdf/02sr005.pdf
6. Wu, Z., Christensen, D., Li, M., Wang, Q.: A Survey of CMM/CMMI Implementation in China. In: Li, M., Boehm, B., Osterweil, L.J. (eds.) SPW 2005. LNCS, vol. 3840, pp. 507–520. Springer, Heidelberg (2006)
7. Appraisal Assistant, http://www.sqi.gu.edu.au/AppraisalAssistant/indexFrameset.html
8. CMMI® Appraisal Recorder, http://www.se-cure.ch/Products.html
9. Interim Maturity Evaluation based on Capability Maturity Model Integration for Development (CMMI-DEV), V1.2, Management Information System, http://www.man-info-systems.com/index_files/FreeTools.htm
10. CMMiPal 1.0, Chemuturi Consultants, http://www.brothersoft.com/cmmipal-63969.html
11. Software Engineering Institute (SEI): Standard CMMI Appraisal Method for Process Improvement (SCAMPI), Version 1.1: Method Definition Document, Handbook, CMU/SEI-2001-HB-001, Carnegie Mellon University, Pittsburgh (2001)

Predicting Fault-Prone Modules: A Comparative Study

Hao Jia[1,2], Fengdi Shu[1], Ye Yang[1], and Qing Wang[1]

[1] Laboratory for Internet Software Technologies, Institute of Software,
The Chinese Academy of Sciences, Beijing 100190, China
[2] Graduate University of Chinese Academy of Sciences,
19# Yuquan Road, Shijingshan District, Beijing 100039, P.R. China
{jiahao,fdshu,ye,wq}@itechs.iscas.ac.cn

Abstract. Offshore and outsourced software development is a rapidly increasing trend in global software business environment. Predicting fault-prone modules in outsourced software product may allow both parties to establish mutually satisfactory, cost-effective testing strategies and product acceptance criteria, especially in iterative transitions. In this paper, based on industrial software releases data, we conduct an empirical study to compare ten classifiers over eight sets of code attributes, and provide recommendations to aid both the client and vendor to assess the products' quality through defect prediction. Overall, a generally high accuracy is observed, which confirms the usefulness of the metric-based classification. Furthermore, two classification techniques, Random Forest and Bayesian Belief Network, outperform the others in terms of predictive accuracy; in more detail, the former is the most cost-effective and the latter is of the lowest fault-prone module escaping rate. Our study also concludes that code metrics including size, traditional complexity, and object-oriented complexity perform fairly well.

1 Introduction

The last two decades have witnessed an increasingly prominent trend toward the offshore and outsourced software development. However, quality is difficult to measure and control when a project is performed outsourced [1]. Theoretically, the client and vendor should share the responsibilities for managing the quality of outsourced projects. While practically, problems arise partially due to the vendor's motives for maximizing profits and the client's lack of control and visibility into the vendor's quality control processes. To make matters worse, such problems are sometimes ignored in the software outsourcing literature [2].

One goal of defect prediction techniques is to identify high-risk modules and get desirable testing efficiency based on historical records. It can be leveraged to mitigate these "outsourced" problems by aiding the vendor in making strategic test plans and the client in accordingly monitoring the test plans before making acceptance and deployment decisions, especially in iterative and incremental transitions, which are prevalently adopted. Previous research on defect prediction mainly focuses on the competitive performance of prediction models over predictors such as software metrics [3, 7]. A number of prediction models are proposed to predict either the type

O. Gotel, M. Joseph, and B. Meyer (Eds.): SEAFOOD 2009, LNBIP 35, pp. 45–59, 2009.

of a module (whether it is fault-prone or not) or the number of faults within a module [3, 4, 5]. The former is usually referred to as classification models while the latter is usually referred to as regression models; and the two kinds of models have commonly different performance indicators. Besides, various types of metrics have been proposed including product metrics, process metrics, deployment and usage metrics, and software and hardware configurations metrics [6]. A group of theoretical and empirical studies have been conducted to compare the predictive performance of assorted prediction models [3, 4, 5, 7, 8, 9] over diverse metrics [10, 11, 12] under different predictive indicators [19]. However, no convergent conclusion has been drawn on some model's superiority over another over all data sets [31].

Our study aims to provide useful recommendations on the selection of prediction models and software metrics for both the client and vendor to better control the quality of the outsourced software. Especially, due to the increasing trends of market changes and company's growth, more and more clients favor iterative and incremental transitions of outsourced software to increase their abilities in operational flexibility and scaling. Therefore, we pay particular attention to predicting fault-prone modules in the context of consecutive releases. As a result, the conclusions are based on comparisons of ten classification models over eight sets of code metrics based on data from three releases of an industrial software project. We choose the compared classification models and code metrics with respect to three major considerations: 1) Classification has been proven to be a promising technique in achieving better software quality control [3, 7]. 2) Because clients lack technical expertise and have limited understandable sources, we apply code metrics and historical defect data that can be collected automatically by tools without in-depth technical knowledge needed. 3) Considering the frequent tradeoff between cost and quality, different defect prediction models should be adopted according to business value propositions.

The remainder of the paper is organized as follows: Section 2 presents some related work; Section 3 deals with the experimental setup; Section 4 reports and analyzes the major results and provides corresponding recommendations; Section 5 discusses the threats to validity; and finally Section 6 draws the conclusions and discusses the future work.

2 Related Work

Predicting which modules are more fault-prone than others has been addressed by a lot number of research, among which have assessed the predictive performance of some classification models over various metrics across a large number of accuracy indicators.

2.1 Classification Models for Predicting Fault-Prone Modules

A wide range of classifiers have been developed and applied to predict fault-prone modules in software. Basili et al. [13] used **Logistic Regression (LR)** to predict the fault-prone classes on a suite of object-oriented design metrics. Fenton et al. [14] proposed **Bayesian Belief Networks (BBN)** for software defect prediction. Guo et al. [15] and Lessmann et al. [7] proposed **Random Forest (RF)** classifier for defect prediction on NASA MDP defect datasets [1]. By comparing with some machine learning and statistical methods, they found that its accuracy was generally higher. Xing et al. [16] adopted **Support Vector Machine (SVM)** as predictive classification model for a Medical Imaging System and achieved better predictive performance than discriminant analysis and CART. Elish et al. [17] further substantiated the attractiveness of SVM on MDP dataset. Recently, Menzies et al. [10] pointed out that a **Naive Bayes (NB)** model was easy to interpret as well as computationally efficient. Moser et al. [18] observed the performance of Naïve Bayes, J48 Decision Tree and Logistic Regression respectively, and proposed that **J48 Decision Tree (JDT)** learner generated very accurate results for the three releases of the Eclipse project.

However, as Myrtveit et al. [31] mentioned, "empirical studies on software prediction models do not converge with respect to the question 'which prediction model is best'". Therefore, our study uses industrial project data to compare ten prediction models on eight sets of predictors, aim to develop further understanding to improve the convergence and formulate useful recommendations to facilitate their application to outsourced software projects in similar developing context.

2.2 Code Metrics as Predictors

Another essential factor influencing the predictive performance is the software metrics as predictors. The most studied and traditional approach for defect prediction is to relate software defects to the product itself. Along these lines there have been various studies. The most traditional ones are size and complexity [21, 22]. To measure the span-new characteristics of object-oriented programs, Chidamber and Kemerer [23] proposed a suite of object-oriented design metrics (CK metrics), which has been substantiated by several theoretical and empirical studies [13, 24]. Moreover, other code metrics are proposed to complement CK metrics in defect prediction. Zimmermann et al. [26] extracted a vast amount of size and untypical complexity metrics from source code of Eclipse project and found a significant correlation between their metrics and pre- and post-release defects. Nagappan and Ball [27] showed that the software defect density can be effectively predicted by relative code churn. Additionally, Nagappan et al. [11] identified a number of code metrics in terms of modules to predict post-release failures within five Microsoft projects, and turned out that complexity metrics can be successful predictors.

In all, as Menzies et al. [10] demonstrated, code metrics are useful, easy to use, and widely used. Based on the experiments on eight subsystems taken from four systems, they found that the predictors got from source code performed surprisingly well.

2.3 Performance Measures for Assessing Classification Models

Classification models are routinely assessed by counting the number of correctly predicted modules over hold-out data. El-Eman et al. [19] described a large number of performance indicators which can be constructed from four basic figures in confusion matrix [20] shown in Table 1. When applied to defect prediction, "yes" means fault-prone, and "no" means not fault-prone. Accuracy, precision, and recall are three of the commonly used performance indicators [20].

---

[1] NASA Data Program. http://mdp.ivv.nasa.gov/

Table 1. Confusion matrix

		Predicted Class	
		yes	No
Actual Class	yes	True Positive (TP)	False Negative (FN)
	no	False Positive (FP)	True Negative (TN)

Accuracy is also known as correct classification rate. This is an intuitively appealing measure of predictive performance since it is easy to interpret and has been widely used in a number of previous studies [10, 16, 17]. It is calculated as follows:

$$Accuracy = \frac{TP + TN}{TP + TN + FP + FN}$$

Precision is also known as correctness. The higher the precision, the less effort and resources is taken in activities, like testing and inspection, on not fault-prone modules. It is calculated as follows:

$$Precision = \frac{TP}{TP + FP}$$

Recall is also known as defect detection rate. The higher the recall, the fewer fault-prone modules go undetected. It is calculated as follows:

$$Recall = \frac{TP}{TP + FN}$$

3   Study Design

The steps of this comparative study include:

- Identifying candidate classification models, sets of code metrics, and performance indicators;
- Preparing data; (w.r.t. parameter initialization of the selected models, historical defect data of the subject system, and code metric data obtained automatically);
- Producing and recording of prediction results;
- Comparing and analyzing results;
- Providing recommendations;

3.1 Subject System

The comparative study makes use of defect data and program code from three consecutive releases of a software project within a medium-sized software organization in China. The lead product is the software quality management platform (QMP) [25], targeting to facilitate the process improvement initiatives in many small and medium software organizations. It is a web application using Java programming language and Servlet/Struts/Hibernate architecture. The core products features incrementally and iteratively offered by the project series.

General information about the three consecutive releases is shown in Table 2. For reasons of confidentiality, we shall refer to them as release A, B, and C, using the alphabetical order stands for their release sequence. All of the releases were developed and tested by relatively steady teams under similar environment. In our study, *experienced developers* are defined as the ones with more than three years experiences in developing web applications using Java. The development team also included several graduated students with about two-year experiences in software development. QMP was tested independently of developers, and the column *team size* merely indicates the number of developers involving no reviewers or testers. Furthermore, to evaluate the performance of classification models for the latest release from historical data, we use prior releases A and B for model building and the latest release C for performance estimation.

Table 2. Brief information about the three releases of QMP

Release	# Source Files	# Classes and Interfaces	Lines of Code	Project duration (months)	Team size	# Experienced developers
A	719	910	111,257	5	13	5
B	736	940	114,129	1	5	4
C	909	1154	148,210	4	7	6

3.2 Candidate Classification Models, Code Metric Sets, and Performance Indicators

3.2.1 Classification Models

This study aims at contrasting the competitive performance of various classification models and sets of metrics. To that end, an overall number of 10 classifiers are selected. The selection aims at achieving a balance between classical defect prediction models (i.e., Naïve Bayes, Bayesian Belief Network, SVM, K-Nearest Neighbor, Decision Tree, Random Forest, and Logistic Regression), and novel approaches that have not yet found widespread usage in defect prediction (i.e., neural network techniques like Multi-Layer Perceptron and Radial Basis Function Networks, and ensemble methods like LogitBoost). A detailed description of most methods can be found in general textbooks like [20].

3.2.2 Code Metric Sets

For each of the modules, we use following two metrics tools and several scripts to extract code metrics automatically from the Java source files of the subject system:

- Understand for Java[2] (UJ) by Scientific Toolworks.
- SourceMonitor[3] (SM) by Campwood Software.

---

[2] Scientific Toolworks. http://www.scitools.com
[3] Campwood Software. http://www.campwoodsw.com/

We choose these tools from the collection of implements employed in [6, 28] according to whether they are available (license purchased or open sourced), easy to use, of relatively high performance, and applicable to our dataset. These tools collect eight sets of metrics data: Understand for Java extracts five sets and SourceMonitor extracts three sets. Details may be referred to Section 3.4.3.

3.2.3 Performance Indicators

As we discussed in Section 1, quality prediction models in offshore and outsourced software development should not only be useful but also applicable to different business value propositions. We use accuracy to indicate the usefulness of classification models over predictors. As for applicability, precision and recall are used according to different business value propositions. In more detail, for example, high-assurance and complex mission-critical systems should be taken under more intensive testing at the expense of cost and schedule, which requiring high recall; while for market-oriented software systems, their success depend mainly on the chances and requirements of market and moderate flaws might be tolerated and fixed in updated releases, which preferring to high precision. Moreover, this study assesses the competitive performance using nonparametric tests, which is distribution-free and reportedly robust to outliers [7].

3.3 Preparation of Data

3.3.1 Parameter Initialization of the Selected Models

We used the open-source WEKA[4] machine learning toolkit to conduct this study. Except for C-SVC, where grid search was used to check the candidate parameters and explore the best performance, other classification models were initialized according to parameters used in prior work [17]. Details are listed as follows:

- NB (Naïve Bayes): it needs no parameter.
- BBN (Bayesian Belief Network): the Simple Estimator algorithm is used for finding the conditional probability tables and the K2 algorithm is used for searching the network.
- C-SVC (C-Support Vector Classification): it is one type of support vector machines used for classification. The kernel function used is radial basis function; regularization parameter (C) is set at 1; bandwidth (γ) is set at 0.5.
- LR (logistic regression): it is set with default parameters.
- MLP (Multi-Layer Perceptron): it is a network architecture using a three layered, fully connected, and feed-forward multi-Layer perceptron. MLP is trained using back-propagation algorithm. The number of hidden nodes is set at 3. All nodes in the network used the sigmoid transfer function. The learning rate is initially 0.3 and the momentum term is set at 0.2. The algorithm is halted when there is no significant reduction in training error for 500 epochs with a tolerance value to convergence of 0.01.
- RBFNet (Radial Basis Function Network): it uses the k-means clustering algorithm to determine the Gaussians RBF center c and width σ. The value of k is set at 2.

---

[4] WEKA: http://www.cs.waikato.ac.nz/~ml/weka/

- KNN-3 (*K*-Nearest Neighbor): the number of observations (k) is set at 3.
- LogitBoost: it is an algorithm performing additive logistic regression to classify using a regression scheme as the base learner. Threshold on improvement in likelihood is set at -1.8; no internal cross-validation is performed; the number of iterations to be performed is set at 10.
- J48 (C4.5 Decision Tree): the confidence factor used for pruning is set at 25% and the minimum number of instances per leaf is set at 2.
- RF (Random Forest): it incorporates CART as base learner. The number of trees to be generated is set at 10; the number of attributes to be used in random selection and the maximum depth of the trees are unlimited.

In addition, the merit of a particular classification model is estimated on the hold-out test set (so-called split-sample setup [7]).

3.3.2 Historical Defect Data

Problems are systematically recorded by the bug management tool. To assess the delivered products' quality, we are interested in both pre- and post-release defects – that are, defects typically discovered during software testing and inspection, and those resulting in failures in the field and reported by users [11].

For each release, the defect data are reported and grouped according to their locations in terms of **modules**, which comprise of a few source files each of which includes a series of classes. We thus could assign each module the number of defects. The definition criterion of fault-prone module should be set according to specific context. In our study, considering a large part of modules (e.g., 16% modules in release B) contain no defect, we define fault-prone module according to: rank modules per release according to the descending order of the number of defects, categorize the top modules taking up the eighty percent of total defects into fault-prone and the others non-fault-prone. Information on defects and modules of per release is shown in Table 3.

Table 3. Brief information about defects and modules per release

Release	# Defects	# Modules	# Fault-proneness	Range of module size (LOC)
A	657	30	13	162~57367
B	119	31	7	162~57531
C	998	37	12	289~74266

3.3.3 Automatically Extracting Code Metric Data

In this work, sets of code metrics were adopted according to two criteria: 1) automatically collected requiring little technical background; and 2) covering major size and complexity (traditional and OO complexity) metrics.

For reason of space constraint, the full sets of metrics are neglected. UJ collects metrics at module and class levels; SM at module and file levels. In order to have all metrics apply to modules, we summarized the file and class metrics across each module. For each file and class metric X, we computed the average and the maximum value per module (henceforth denoted as *X_Mean* and *X_Max*, respectively). Taking metric CountLineCode, the number of lines of code per class, as an example,

CountLineCode _Max metric indicates the length of the largest class in a module, and *CountLineCode _Mean*, the mean of CountLineCode for all classes in a module.

To evaluate the predictive performance of metrics computed by different tools at different granularity level - module, class, and file, we partition the metrics data into eight sets shown in Table 4. Since code metrics at class level in the full set (UJ-3) are partially overlapped, UJ-2 is constructed using mean and max values of 20 metrics selected from UJ-1 to remove potential redundancy and irrelevance. UJ-4, UJ-5, and SM-3 are used to verify the hypothesis that a combination of metrics from different viewpoints can arrive at better predictive accuracy.

Table 4. Sets of metrics data

Metrics data collected by UJ	Metrics data collected by SM
UJ-1: values of total 11 metrics per module	SM-1: values of total 23 metrics per module
UJ-2: mean and max values of selected 20 metrics per class	SM-2: mean and max values of total 24 metrics per file
UJ-3: mean and max values of total 39 metrics per class	SM-3: combination of SM-1 and SM-2
UJ-4: combination of UJ-1 and UJ-2	
UJ-5: combination of UJ-1 and UJ-3	

4   Results and Analysis

4.1   Summary of Results

We apply the ten classification models to predict fault-prone modules using all eight sets of metrics data respectively. All the predictions are carried out by WEKA with uniform input data rapidly (less than 1 second), and there is no observable differences on learning effort and ease of use among these models and metrics sets. Accuracy, basically indicating the predictive performance, is displayed in Table 5, while results on precision and recall are neglected due to space limitation. The classifier yielding the best results for a particular data set is highlighted in boldface, and the metrics data

Table 5. Predictive accuracy on hold-out test data

Model	UJ-1	UJ-2	UJ-3	UJ-4	UJ-5	SM-1	SM-2	SM-3
BBN	**0.8333**	*0.8667*	0.8333	0.8333	*0.8667*	**0.8333**	0.8000	**0.8333**
NB	*0.8333*	0.7667	0.8000	0.8000	0.8000	0.7333	0.7333	0.7333
C-SVC	*0.6333*	*0.6333*	*0.6333*	*0.6333*	*0.6333*	0.6000	0.6000	*0.6333*
LR	0.7667	0.8000	0.6667	*0.9000*	0.6333	0.5667	0.8333	0.7333
MLP	**0.8333**	0.8667	0.8667	*0.9000*	**0.8667**	0.6667	0.7667	0.7333
RBFNet	0.7000	0.8000	0.7667	*0.8667*	0.8333	0.6333	0.7667	0.6667
KNN-3	0.8000	*0.9000*	0.8667	0.8667	**0.8667**	0.7333	**0.8333**	0.8000
LogitBoost	0.7000	*0.8000*	0.7333	0.7667	0.7333	0.7333	0.7333	0.7333
J48	0.8000	0.7333	0.7000	0.7333	0.7000	*0.8333*	0.7000	0.7667
RF	**0.8333**	*0.9000*	**0.8667**	0.8667	**0.8667**	**0.8333**	0.8000	**0.8333**

yielding the best results for a particular classifier is highlighted in italics. What's more, the figure is based on hold-out test data (release C); results on training data are neglected for brevity.

4.2 Comparisons of Classification Models

We compare the classifiers' predictive performance over all eight data sets, which is meaningful to avoid their bias toward certain metrics data. To evaluate individual classification models and verify if some are generally superior to others, we conduct Friedman test to check whether the differences in performance are significant. All of the p-values for accuracy, precision, and recall fall below 0.05 (the largest value is 1.88E-06). This provides very strong evidence against the assumption that these classifiers give equal performance. Consequently, we proceed with pairwise comparisons to detect which particular classifiers differ significantly. Fig. 1 delineates the results of Wilcoxon signed-rank test (α=0.05) in accuracy using a modified version of Demsar's significance diagram: the diagram plots methods in discussion against mean ranks (calculated by formula in [7]), whereby all methods are sorted according to their ranks given by Friedman test. The line segment to the right of each classifier represents its corresponding critical difference. That is, the left end of the line indicates from which mean rank onward another method is outperformed significantly. For illustrative purposes, this threshold is highlighted with a vertical dotted line. The numbers in horizontal axis indicate mean ranks across all datasets.

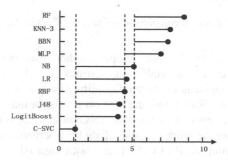

Fig. 1. Results of pairwise comparisons of all classifiers in accuracy

Most classifiers - with few exceptions like C-SVC - achieve promising predictive performance, i.e. accuracy higher than 0.70, precision higher than 0.75, and recall higher than 0.58. Overall, the high level of predictive performance across all classification models confirms the verdict of the general appropriateness of classification models to predict fault-prone models [3, 7].

As for accuracy, it can be observed that RF ranks first and significantly outperforms most of others; it reaches the highest accuracy on six out of eight datasets. The results confirm previous findings [8, 11] regarding the appealing performance of RF for predicting fault-proneness. Since the findings are verified widely on several projects using different metrics, it is recommended to adopt this classifier as one of the best candidates for industrial applications. However, the performance of C-SVC is not as good as what was observed [16, 17]. In our study, it has the lowest ranks in every metric set, and is outperformed critically by all the other classifiers. According to Hsu [30], this phenomenon might be caused by two reasons. One is the usage of RBF kernel because it is proved to be inefficient when the number of features is very large. However, compared to the test data with 46237 features in [30], the largest set of our metrics data consists of only 89 features. So it is unconvincing that the RBF kernel is the fuse. The other possible reason is that the model overfits the training data. After we apply grid search approach on C and γ for UJ-2 using cross-validation, recommended in [30], predictive accuracy is enhanced to 0.6803, still less than 0.7. Further study is needed to explain this phenomenon.

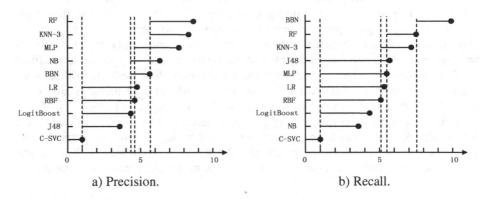

a) Precision.   b) Recall.

Fig. 2. Results of pairwise comparisons of all classifiers in precision and recall

As specified in Section 2.3, we adopt another two performance indicators, precision and recall, to provide viable suggestions on allocating testing resources considering different emphasis on cost or quality. From their significance diagrams shown in Fig. 2, Random Forest with the highest precision may be applied to market-oriented systems; organizations in need of mission-critical systems may be yet in favor of Bayesian Belief Network because of its best performance in recall. It is also noticed that precision and recall of C-SVC are both unsatisfactory over all data sets, since it predicts no fault-prone module, no matter whether there actually is or not.

Several factors contribute to the merits of RF and BBN [7, 29]. In general, both of them provide an experimental way to detect metrics interactions. Specifically, RF is fast to train, robust toward parameter settings, and naturally understandable. Besides, it estimates the importance of metrics. As for BBN, it uses probabilistic models rather than just the input features directly.

4.3 Comparisons of Metrics Data

Another goal of our study is to compare the impact of diverse automatically-extracted code metrics data on defect prediction. To reduce bias introduced by the classifier, we compare predictive performance of all classifiers over each metrics data set. Friedman test is used to detect the differences among metrics data sets in accuracy, precision, and recall. Significant difference is only found for accuracy with p-value<0.05, while p-values for precision and recall (>0.05) indicate little or no evidence against the null hypothesis. Hence, the discussion of metrics data below is based on accuracy, and the discrepancies in performance measured by recall and precision are neglected.

Furthermore, results of pairwise comparisons in accuracy are depicted in Fig. 3. Similar to the discussion of classification models in section 4.2, the predictive performance based on these sets are generally appealing. Generally speaking, predictive accuracy based on metrics data collected by UJ exceeds – with few exceptions – that of those collected by SM. Specifically, UJ-2, UJ-5, and UJ-4 outperform their competitors significantly with possibly random differences among them three.

First, we evaluate the impact of combination of metrics on predictive performance. On one hand, UJ-2 has significantly higher accuracy than its superset UJ-3. The same relation exists between UJ-3 and UJ-5, and UJ-1 and UJ-5. This result, according to our dataset, denies the hypothesis that larger set of metrics leading to better predictive performance. On the other hand, the performances of UJ-2 and its superset, UJ-4, behave no evident difference. Similarly, SM-3 outperforms its subset SM-2 significantly, but behaves insignificantly better than its another subset SM-1. Therefore, we cannot confirm that larger set of metrics is doomed to lose in defect prediction. To check the impact of multicollinearity caused by combination, we further adopt principle components analysis. But no evident enhancement or degradation in predictive performance is observed.

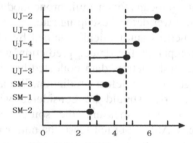

Fig. 3. Results of pairwise comparisons of all metrics sets in accuracy

Then, we investigate the reasons for better performance of metrics data collected by UJ and, find out that types of metrics may be a possible explanation. It is observed that SM collects most metrics of size and traditional complexity (i.e. McCabe's cyclomatic complexity), but few of object-oriented properties are concerned. Whereas, UJ reach a balance among three kinds of metrics including size, traditional complexity, and object-oriented complexity (i.e. some of CK metrics) by measuring features like coupling between classes and weighted methods per class.

4.4 Recommendations

The analysis results led us to conclude a set of recommendations to aid both the client and vendor to assess the products' quality through defect prediction in offshore and outsourced software development:

- Business Considerations. Defect prediction provides a comprehensive approach for the clients to participate in the formal quality control process. It facilitates both parties to explore and make detailed contract agreements on quality, aids the vendor to making more strategic test plans, and provides the client with more effective vendor governance on test to make informed decisions.
- Model Usage. Classification models are appropriate to predict the fault-prone modules for quality control. It supports the effective assignment of testing effort and resources to evaluate the quality of delivered software products, by paying particular stress on high-risk modules.
- Model Selection. Based on our study, the predictive accuracy of the 10 classifiers is generally satisfying, among which the Random Forest is the best while C-SVC behaves not so well. Moreover, illustrated by the relevance of statistical hypothesis testing, the discrepancy of the classification models on performance should not be underestimated.
- Cost-effective Consideration. If the customized application is market-oriented, for the client, mostly the costs for fixing defects in later releases are not as high as those for losing the potential market. Random Forest is recommended for this kind of software because of its highest accuracy and precision.
- Quality Consideration. When comes to high-assurance and mission-critical systems, particular stress should be paid to quality consideration. A field defect may result in a great loss and even calamity. In this context, Bayesian Belief Network is more competent. Due to our study, it performs the highest recall and desirable accuracy, which means fewer fault-prone modules will be misclassified as non-fault-prone and lower defects escaping rate.
- Code Metrics. Code metrics automatically gained by Understand for Java and SourceMonitor are competent for defect prediction with no further technical support in need. In general, metrics data collected by Understand for Java may serve as more sound ground for defect prediction. We also propose that object-oriented complexity metrics should be considered with size and traditional complexity metrics to better measure the source code in object-oriented programming languages. At last but not least, the number of predictors of a set is not definitely proportional to the predictive performance.

5 Threats to Validity

Drawing general conclusions from empirical studies in software engineering is difficult because any process depends on numerous potentially relevant context factors. As for the generalization of results, the used dataset is a possible source of bias, e.g., its measurement accuracy and representativeness [18]. To guarantee the measurement accuracy, we verified the data from QMP through reading related documents, interviewing with team members, and so on. In our study, the subject project was in-house, written in Java, and iteratively developed. Hence, the conclusions and recommendations may be not transferable to all other kinds of projects. However, since the results of this study are in line with a number of observations made by other researchers, we are confident that the obtained results are relevant for the software defect prediction community.

The selection of classifiers is another possible source of threat. Given the variety of available learning algorithms, there are still others that could have been considered. Our selection is guided by the aim of finding a balance between classical techniques and novel approaches. We believe that the most important representatives are included.

Finally, it should be noted that classification is only a single step within a multistage defect prediction process [10]. Especially, data preprocessing or engineering activities such as the removal of redundant and irrelevant features may improve the predictive performance. A wide range of different methods for data transformation and feature selection have already been proposed in the data mining literature. As our results indicate that most classification models already achieve promising predictive performance, i.e., accuracy higher than 0.70, precision higher than 0.75, and recall higher than 0.58, we left these preprocessing activities for future investigation.

6 Conclusions and Future Work

In offshore and outsourced software development, lack of technical know-how weakens the client's ability to keep track of the vendor's quality control processes. It is beneficial for both parties to reach the consensus on quality in accordance with the client's business value propositions. Therefore, our study aims to provide useful recommendations on the defect prediction approaches to aid the vendor in making strategic test plans and the client in accordingly monitoring test plan before making acceptance and deployment decisions. Furthermore, due to the prevalent trends of iterative and incremental transition of outsourced software aiming at the ubiquitous changes in market, we focus on the defect prediction in the context of consecutive releases.

This study focuses on the selection of prediction models and software metrics for both parties to better predict the quality of the releases. We choose and compare 10 classification models over 8 sets of code metrics based on three releases of an industrial software project. Our study concludes that: classification models are appropriate to predict the fault-prone modules for quality control; for the trade-off between quality and cost in defect prediction, Random Forest is the most cost-effective and Naïve Bayes Network is of the highest detection rate of fault-prone modules; predictive performance based on automatically-gained code metrics is appealing; object-oriented complexity metrics should be considered with size and traditional complexity metrics to better measure the source code in object-oriented programming languages.

Future work includes extension of current study in three respects:

- Extending the scope of analysis to cover more classification models and projects.
- Exploring the impact of diverse input features on the predictive performance.
- Analyzing the effects of data preprocessing and feature selection methods for defect prediction.

Acknowledgments. This work is supported by the National Natural Science Foundation of China under grant Nos. 60573082, 90718042; the National Hi-Tech Research and Development Plan of China under Grant No. 2006AA01Z182, 2007AA010303; the National Key Technologies R&D Program under Grant No. 2007CB310802.

References

1. Sommer, C., Troxler, G.: Outsourcing and Offshoring: The Consultancies Estimates. In: Meyer, B., Joseph, M. (eds.) SEAFOOD 2007. LNCS, vol. 4716, pp. 109–113. Springer, Heidelberg (2007)
2. Sabherwal, R.: The evolution of coordination in outsourced software development projects: a comparison of client and vendor perspectives. Information and Organization 13, 153–202 (2003)
3. Khoshgoftaar, T.M., Seliya, N.: Comparative Assessment of Software Quality Classification Techniques: An Empirical Case Study. Empirical Software Engineering 9, 229–257 (2004)
4. Khoshgoftaar, T.M., Seliya, N.: Fault Prediction Modeling for Software Quality Estimation: Comparing Commonly Used Techniques. Empirical Software Engineering 8, pp. 255–283 (2003)
5. Zhong, S., Khoshgoftaar, T.M., Seliya, N.: Analyzing Software Measurement Data with Clustering Techniques. IEEE Intelligent Systems 19, 20–27 (2004)
6. Li, P.L., Herbsleb, J., Shaw, M.: Finding Predictors of Field Defects for Open Source Software Systems in Commonly Available Data Sources: a Case Study of OpenBSD. In: Proc. IEEE Software Metrics Symp., pp. 10–32. IEEE Computer Society, Washington (2005)
7. Lessmann, S., Baesens, B., Mues, C., Pietsch, S.: Benchmarking classification models for software defect prediction: A proposed framework and novel findings. IEEE Trans. SW Eng. 34, 485–496 (2008)
8. Lanubile, F., Visaggio, G.: Evaluating predictive quality models derived from software measures: lessons learned. J. Systems and Software 38, 225–234 (1997)
9. Fenton, N., Neil, M.: A critique of software defect prediction models. IEEE Trans. SW Eng. 25, 675–689 (1999)
10. Menzies, T., Greenwald, J., Frank, A.: Data Mining Static Code Attributes to Learn Defect Predictors. IEEE Trans. Software Eng. 33, 2–13 (2007)
11. Nagappan, N., Ball, N., Zeller, A.: Mining metrics to predict component failures. In: Proc. International Conference on Software engineering, pp. 452–461. ACM, New York (2006)
12. Schneidewind, N.F.: Methodology for Validating Software Metrics. IEEE Trans. Software Eng. 18, 410–422 (1992)
13. Basili, V., Briand, L., Melo, W.: A validation of object-oriented design metrics as quality indicators. IEEE Trans. Software Eng. 22, 751–761 (1996)
14. Fenton, N., Neil, M., Krause, P.: Software measurement: uncertainty and causal modeling. IEEE Software 19, 116–122 (2002)
15. Guo, L., Ma, Y., Cukic, B., Singh, H.: Robust prediction of fault-proneness by random forests. In: Proc. International Symposium on Software Reliability Engineering (ISSRE 2004), pp. 417–428. IEEE Computer Society, Washington (2004)

16. Xing, X., Guo, P., Lyu, M.R.: A Novel Method for Early Software Quality Prediction Based on Support Vector Machine. In: Proc. International Symposium on Software Reliability Engineering, pp. 213–222. IEEE Computer Society, Washington (2005)
17. Elish, K.O., Elish, M.O.: Predicting defect-prone software modules using support vector machines. J. Systems and Software 81, 649–660 (2008)
18. Moser, R., Pedrycz, W., Succi, G.: A comparative analysis of the efficiency of change metrics and static code attributes for defect prediction. In: Proc. international conference on Software engineering, pp. 181–190. ACM, New York (2008)
19. El-Emam, K., Benlarbi, S., Goel, N., Rai, S.N.: Comparing Case-Based Reasoning Classifiers for Predicting High-Risk Software Components. J. Systems and Software 55, 301–320 (2001)
20. Witten, I., Frank, E.: Data Mining: Practical Machine Learning Tools and Techniques, 2nd edn. Morgan Kaufmann, San Francisco (2005)
21. McCabe, T.: A Complexity Measure. IEEE Trans. Software Eng. 2, 308–320 (1976)
22. Halstead, M.: Elements of Software Science. Elsevier, Amsterdam (1977)
23. Chidamber, S., Kemerer, C.: A metrics suite for object-oriented design. IEEE Trans. Software Eng. 20(6), 476–493 (1994)
24. Subramanyam, R., Krishnan, M.S.: Empirical Analysis of CK Metrics for Object-Oriented Design Complexity: Implications for Software Defects. IEEE Trans. Software Eng. 29, 297–310 (2003)
25. Yang, Y., Li, Q., Li, M., Wang, Q.: An Empirical Analysis on Distribution Patterns of Software Maintenance Effort. In: Proc. International Conference of Software Maintenance, pp. 456–459. IEEE Computer Society, Washington (2008)
26. Zimmermann, T., Premraj, R., Zeller, A.: Predicting Defects for Eclipse. In: Proc. International Workshop on Predictor Models in Software Engineering, p. 9. IEEE Computer Society, Washington (2007)
27. Nagappan, N., Ball, T.: Use of relative code churn measures to predict system defect density. In: Proc. International Conference on Software Engineering, pp. 284–292. ACM, New York (2005)
28. Wu, S., Wang, Q., Yang, Y.: Quantitative Analysis of Faults and Failures with Multiple Releases of SoftPM. In: Proc. International Symposium on Empirical Software Engineering and Measurement, pp. 198–205. ACM, New York (2008)
29. Challagulla, V.U.B., Bastani, F.B., Yen, I.-L., Paul, R.A.: Empirical Assessment of Machine Learning based Software Defect Prediction Techniques. In: Proc. International Workshop on Object-Oriented Real-Time Dependable Systems, pp. 263–270. IEEE Computer Society, Washington (2005)
30. Hsu, C.-W., Chang, C.-C., Lin, C.-J.: A practical guide to support vector classification (2003), http://www.csie.ntu.edu.tw/~cjlin/libsvm/
31. Myrtveit, I., Stensrud, E., Shepperd, M.: Reliability and Validity in Comparative Studies of Software Prediction Models. IEEE Trans. Software Eng. 31, 380–391 (2005)

Effort Drivers Estimation for Brazilian Geographically Distributed Software Development

Ana Carina M. Almeida[1,2], Renata Souza[1], Gibeon Aquino[1,2], and Silvio Meira[1,2]

[1] Federal University of Pernambuco (UFPE) - Informatics Center
Recife – PE – Brasil
{acma2,rmcrs,gsaj,srlm}@cin.ufpe.br
[2] Centro de Estudos e Sistemas Avançados do Recife (C.E.S.A.R)
Rua Bione, 220 - Bairro do Recife – CEP 50030-390
Recife - PE – Brasil
{ana.almeida,gibeon.aquino,silvio}@cesar.org.br

Abstract. To meet the requirements of today's fast paced markets, it is important to develop projects on time and with the minimum use of resources. A good estimate is the key to achieve this goal. Several companies have started to work with geographically distributed teams due to cost reduction and time-to-market. Some researchers indicate that this approach introduces new challenges, because the teams work in different time zones and have possible differences in culture and language. It is already known that the multisite development increases the software cycle time. Data from 15 DSD projects from 10 distinct companies were collected. The analysis shows drivers that impact significantly the total effort planned to develop systems using DSD approach in Brazil.

Keywords: Effort Driver, Estimation, Distributed Software Development.

1 Introduction

Over the last decades, many companies have started to work with geographically distributed teams developing software. A lot of advantages encouraged them to implement software in multisite [1]. The main factors that have driven distributed software development (DSD) are:

- Differences in the development cost among offshore centers – The market demand for system development is bigger than the number of engineers available [2], due to the significantly increase of the engineer salary in specify areas as well as the software cost. Besides, some governments subsidize a taxes deduction for companies in order to stimulate Information Technology (IT) business in their countries reducing the software development cost [1], [3].
- Time-to-market – Creating products with teams in different time zones in order to accelerate development time by using the *follow-the-sun* concept [1].
- Qualified and available engineers to develop software [1].
- Staying close to the customer in order to properly know their business and needs [1].

O. Gotel, M. Joseph, and B. Meyer (Eds.): SEAFOOD 2009, LNBIP 35, pp. 60–65, 2009.
© Springer-Verlag Berlin Heidelberg 2009

On the other hand, the DSD approach has many challenges to make the project successful. Mainly for the project managers that need to synchronize the activities and communication among different sites with different time zones, cultural aspects, language and sometimes different development process among sites [1], [4].

It is already known that it is a big challenge to deliver software on time, on budget with all required features and functionalities. The DSD approach increases the management complexity. An accurate estimate can improve the project planning and help the creation of a detailed activities schedule [5], thereby minimizing the risks intrinsic in DSD projects. According to Herbsleb [6] the multisite development requires more effort than centralized development for creating a system with the similar size and complexity, because of reduced communication.

There are few estimation methods that support DSD approach, for example, the COCOMO II method [7]. Unfortunately, the COCOMO II does not introduce all factors that can impact the DSD project duration. The effort driver list can be used to adapt estimation methods and active a better software planning.

The approach taken for this study is based on a combination of data collection (interviews with practitioners), analysis with theoretical research and empirical experience. The result of this paper is an effort drivers list that could increase the project effort in Brazilian multisite development. We analyzed fifteen projects data, from ten different companies, that are being developed geographically distributed in Brazil.

This article is organized as follows: Section 2 describes the sources that impact planning and estimation on DSD projects; section 3 presents the research result and shows an effort drivers list and section 4 explains the expected results of this research and future works.

2   Sources of Effort Drivers Estimation for Geographically Distributed Software Development

As already known the DSD approach introduces new challenges in the software engineering area. In order to have a better project planning for multisite projects it is important to identify the main drivers that can increase the project's effort.

Some researches indicate root causes of the effort deviation. These aspects are described below:

- Communication over distance – Synchronous and asynchronous communication impact the project speed [1], [3]. In DSD projects, the team spends more time on reading/writing emails, conference calls and chatting in order to share or understand information about the project.
- Physical distance, large difference in time zones and small overlap of working hours could delay team communication and more time will be required to solve program issues [3].
- Interdependence among sites – The researches [4] and [8] suggest that the multisite interdependence introduces delay in the resolution of work issue taking more time to develop software. Due to distance it is more difficult to find the right person and establish contact in order to have a collaborative session.

- Cultural fit is another important factor that could impact teams' interaction. What is culture? According to Carmel [3] culture *"(...)provides members with images of their basic concerns, principles, ethics, and bodies of manners, rituals, ideologies, strategies, and tactics of self-survival including certain notions of good deeds and bad,(...)"*.Some authors believe that specific cultural norms regarding software development impacts the way software is created, for example, mind maps [9].
- Architectural Adequacy – It is critical to spend more time in the design phase in order to create decoupled components in the system's architecture as much as feasible in order to be easily distributed among teams [10].
- Project Innovation – A lot of software projects have innovation as a strong requirement. In order to deliver this requirement it is needed to have brainstorming meetings, but geographically distributed it is more difficult and requires more time understanding and challenging ideas between teams. [10]
- Project Turnover - Impacts the planned project effort more when the team is distributed, due to team rebuilding and transferring knowledge [10].

Describing all these sources, it is possible to understand how critical is to consider these risks intrinsic of the DSD context in order to achieve a better software planning.

3   Effort Drivers for Brazilian Distributed Software Development

This section aims to describe the main data collected from project leaders interview regarding Brazilian DSD projects (section 3.1) and show the proposal for an effort drivers list (section 3.2).

3.1   Project Description and Main Questionnaire Results

We interviewed fifteen project leaders (project managers, team and tech leaders) of Brazilian distributed software development from ten unrelated companies. The main purpose of this research is to identify which factors might impact the effort planned on DSD projects in Brazil.

The projects application domains are very diverse, such as, spanning telecommunication, education, finance, government and automotive industry. Some projects are large distributed systems which have 13 sites working together to develop one system. There are also small distributed systems composed by two sites. The teams are allocated in all Brazilian territory, but 34.7% is concentrated in the northeast and 26% in the southeast areas.

Regarding project planning, almost 80% of the companies follow a systematic estimation process. The projects use different methods to estimate, such as Expert Judgment (which is the most used), LOC (Lines of Code) and Use Case Points. It is important to mention that these methods do not have specific drivers for DSD context.

Regarding the main root causes that introduce delay or increase the project effort, the leaders mentioned that need of communication increases substantially the project duration. The project leaders mentioned that more meetings are required to align the teams understanding and to synchronize the project knowledge. The leaders also mentioned that the DSD context pushes the project for using a set of tools that requires team adaptation. The tools most used by them to communicate are mailing list, instant message and conference calls.

Besides that, physical distance, cultural fit and interdependencies among different sites reduce development productivity. Regarding external dependencies among teams, the leaders estimated that at least 10% of the work force was held up due to necessity of information from other sites. The leaders also mentioned that some projects spend more time for the code integration phase than it was expected.

3.2 Effort Driver List for Brazilian DSD

Analyzing the main root causes found in the literature and the feedback from Brazilian leaders about the impact on project duration and effort, it is possible to suggest some effort drivers for DSD projects.

Table 1 presents the effort drivers indentified extracted from theoretical research and interview analyses. The Category column distinguishes the effort driver between: Environment (the driver belongs to DSD context) and Team (the driver belongs to project team). Regarding the source column, it represents the effort driver origin based on theoretical research and interview analyses.

Table 1. Effort Drivers versus sources

ID	Effort Driver	Description / Justification	Category	Source
1	Project sites number	The number of sites that develop the system. The complexity to develop and manage the software increase according with the number of project sites.	Environment	Communication & Interdependence
2	Brazilian Region which the sites are located	The number of Brazilian regions that the sites are located. There are cultural differences among different geographical Brazilian regions.	Environment	Communication & Cultural Fit
3	Communication Support	Diversity of tools used to increase the project productivity allowing a better communication among sites.	Environment	Communication
4	Project Turnover	A high turnover in DSD is more critical than in centralized since constant communication is needed for knowledge transfer.	Team	Project Turnover
5	Project Leader Experience	If the project leader has experience managing DSD projects, he/she has more facility to develop plans for communication, coordination and controlling team activities.	Team	-
6	Team cohesion	In the DSD context it is more difficult to maintain the team cohesion due to physical distance and also cooperation among team members to support each other [2].	Team	Communication & Cultural Fit

Table 2 below represents the possible values that each effort driver can assumes. According to the team or environment feature, it is necessary to select which scale is more adequate for the software that will be developed.

Table 2. Effort Drivers Scale Proposal

ID	Very Low	Low	Nominal	High	Very High
1	Only 2 sites	Between 2 and 3 sites	Between 3 and 4 sites	Between 4 and 5 sites	More than 5 sites
2	One region	Two regions	Three regions	Four regions	Five regions
3			The sites use instant message, email, project mailing list and conference calls.	The sites have project site or wiki and forum.	The developers use multi-user IDE.
4	50%/year	25%/year	20%/year	10%/year	5%/year
5	<3 months	6 months	1 year	3 years	6 years
6	Very Difficult Interaction	Some Difficult Interaction	Basically Cooperative Interactions	Largely Cooperative	Highly Cooperative

4 Conclusions and Future Works

There are a lot of advantages to develop software using DSD approach. On the other hand, it is important to understand the challenges which this approach introduces to achieve the project success.

This paper showed an effort drivers list for DSD context that could support the project planning. This list was proposed from theoretical research, interview analyses based on Brazilian project leaders' response and empirical experience.

During the planning phase, the project leader can use the "Effort Driver Scale" to set the parameters about the project team and DSD environment in a systematic way. It helps to measure the effort needed to develop software. Besides that, at the end of the project, it is possible to compare the effort planned *versus* effort actual in order to understand the effort deviation.

As future work, we intend to create or adapt an estimation method for DSD context in order to support software development planning and increase the estimates accuracy.

References

1. Jorge, A., Rafael, P.: Desenvolvimento Distribuído de Software. Rio de Janeiro, Brasil (2008)
2. Damian, D., Zowghi, D.: The impact of stakeholders? Geographical distribution on managing requirements in a multi-site organization. In: RE, pp. 319–330 (2002)
3. Carmel, E.: Global Software Teams – Collaborating Across Borders and Time-Zones. Prentice Hall, USA

4. Herbsleb, J.D., Audris, M., Thomas, A.F., Rebecca, E.G.: Distance, dependencies, and delay in a global collaboration. ACM, Computer Supported Cooperative Work, Philadelphia (2000)
5. McConnell, S.: Software Estimation - Demystifying the Black Art. Microsoft Press (2006)
6. Herbsleb, J.D., Audris, M., Thomas, A.F., Rebecca, E.G.: An Empirical Study of Speed and Communication in Globally Distributed Software Development. IEEE, IEEE Transactions on Software Engineering (2003)
7. Boehm, B.: Software Cost Estimation with COCOMO II
8. Herbsleb, J.D., Audris, M., Thomas, A.F., Rebecca, E.G.: An Empirical Study Global Software Development: Distance and Speed. In: ACM. Proceedings of the 23rd International Conference on Software Engineering, Toronto, Canada (2001)
9. Hofstede, G.: Cultura e organizações: compreender a nossa programação mental, 1st edn. Edições Silabo, Lisboa (1991)
10. Patrick, K., Daniel, J.P., Raghvinder, S.S.: Cost Estimation for Global Software Development. In: ACM, Proceedings of the 2006 international workshop on Economics driven software engineering research, Shanghai, China (2006)

Challenges for Product Roadmapping in Inter-company Collaboration

Tanja Suomalainen, Maarit Tihinen, and Päivi Parviainen

VTT Technical Research Centre of Finland, Kaitoväylä 1,
P.O. Box 1100, 90571 Oulu, Finland
{Tanja.Suomalainen,Maarit.Tihinen,Paivi.Parviainen}@vtt.fi

Abstract. Product roadmapping is a critical activity in product development, as it provides a link between business aspects and requirements engineering and thus helps to manage a high-level view of the company's products. Nowadays, inter-company collaboration, such as outsourcing, is a common way of developing software products, as through collaboration, organisations gain advantages, such as flexibility with in-house resources, savings in product development costs and gain a physical presence in important markets. The role of product roadmapping becomes even more critical in collaborative settings, since different companies need to align strategies and work together to create products. In order to support companies in improving their own product roadmapping processes, this paper first gives an overview of product roadmapping and then discusses in detail an empirical study of the current practices in industry. The presented results particularly focus on the most challenging and important activities of product roadmapping in collaboration.

Keywords: Product roadmap, roadmapping process, inter-company collaboration, outsourcing.

1 Introduction

Product roadmapping is an approach to planning and defining product requirements, based on market and stakeholders needs. A roadmap is a visualisation of a forecast, which commonly answers a set of "why-what-how-when" questions that generally relate to time, markets, products, and technologies [1]. During product roadmapping, similar activities to requirements engineering (RE) are performed e.g. requirements are elicited, analysed, communicated, agreed, and evolved. The purpose of a product roadmap is to document defined product requirements in a form that is adequate for analysis, communication, and subsequent implementation. However, product roadmapping differs from RE in that it is a process with long-lasting future activities. In product roadmapping, high-level features are presented within a timeline and scheduled for different releases. Instead, in RE, features are analysed in more detail and defined as to what they mean from the perspective of the product development project.

In this paper, product roadmapping is discussed from the inter-company collaboration perspective. Inter-company collaboration or collaboration, as used in this

O. Gotel, M. Joseph, and B. Meyer (Eds.): SEAFOOD 2009, LNBIP 35, pp. 66–80, 2009.

paper, means that two or more parties (e.g. companies, departments, customers, or agencies) work together to create a mutual value and achieve a common goal [2]. Outsourcing is a common way of inter-company collaboration. From this perspective, roadmaps are formal mechanisms for collecting data and sharing information in a partnering environment [3]. A successful roadmap requires the activities of learning and communication, which are also essential to co-operation [4]. In inter-company collaborative product development, a roadmap can help, for example, to select the collaboration partners, since a roadmap can help in estimating what kind of knowledge is needed from outside the organisation. This in turn, enables organisations to concentrate on their core competencies and thus develop products faster and better.

Product roadmapping in inter-company collaboration is a complex and multi-dimensional process. This paper discusses the challenges that inter-company collaboration sets for roadmapping, based on empirical research that has been done during the Merlin[1] project. The study focused on the challenges and opportunities to create product roadmaps in collaboration, including for example, the most important activities to consider, the most typical problems and how those problems can be avoided.

This paper is structured as follows. First, product roadmapping in inter-company collaboration is introduced based on literature research. Second, the empirical research conducted within the Merlin project is described. Then, the empirical findings of the research are presented and, finally, the results are discussed and conclusions are drawn.

2 Collaborative Product Roadmapping Based on Literature

In this section, product roadmapping is introduced. The focus of the section is to describe a general roadmapping process and define the collaboration modes that can be identified in systems and software engineering.

2.1 Product Roadmapping Process

A product roadmap provides a forecast of product family evolution over time and it views relationships between the products [5]. Product roadmaps are generated within the scope of two to three years, during which the roadmaps are revised frequently so that the documents are always current [6]. Product roadmapping is a typically iterative process, which involves a periodic review and improvement of the roadmap based on human interaction, such as face-to-face meetings and workshops [1]. Commonly, product roadmaps are owned by the product owner, who is also responsible for gathering all of the relevant stakeholders to obtain the required information for the roadmaps [7].

Based on literature review conducted in [8], there are several stakeholders in the product roadmapping process. The following functions should at least participate in the process: product management, marketing, development, customer and partner representatives, and engineering. Product roadmapping can be described as a process that includes several iterative cycles, as shown in Figure 1.

---

[1] The Merlin project: Embedded Systems Engineering in Collaboration, 2004-2007.
  URL: http://www.merlinproject.org/

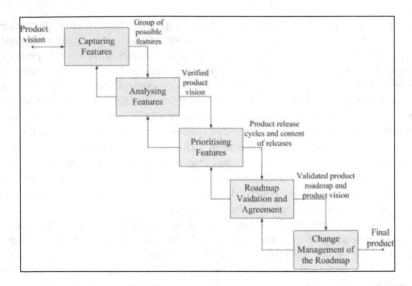

Fig. 1. Product roadmapping process [8]

In the first phase, capturing features, a product vision is identified, product boundaries are set, stakeholders are defined, and product goals are determined. Additionally, based on the market, competitor and customer analysis, major business and market drivers for the product are defined. As a result, all the suggested features in a product are collected and documented in a product roadmap template. In the analysing phase, all collected features are evaluated to remove uncertainty, to resolve conflicts, and to make resource and cost estimations. As a result of this phase, the product vision is revised and captured as a product roadmap, i.e. verified. In the prioritising phase, all collected features are evaluated and put into order of importance, based on the verified product vision. Customers have an important role, since they provide guidelines to the product by expressing their needs and expectations, as well as what they are willing to pay for the product. As a result of prioritisation, the product release cycles are planned and the content of each product releases are defined. In the next phase, the roadmap is validated and thereafter approved. At this point, the members of the roadmapping team shall review whether the process leads to the desired outcome, and if appropriate, take further corrective actions. After validating the product vision and product roadmap, agreements are made between the stakeholders, and the product roadmapping process can be taken forward. The last phase of product roadmapping, change management, is part of the product development. The change management process begins with a change request, i.e. the features to be changed. Thereafter, the change is analysed and impacts of the change are defined, for instance, the scope of the change request is identified. The impact analysis is conducted by the stakeholders of the roadmapping process. Customers and collaboration partners are also involved in the impact analysis. As a result, the changes are implemented and documented.

2.2 Collaboration Modes

Collaboration can take numerous forms and it can be designed for different purposes. This paper focuses on company or inter-company collaboration, in which the co-operation companies share some of their activities [2].

Collaboration modes can be classified in several different ways. In this paper, collaboration modes are divided into the following three categories: joint R&D partnerships, customer-supplier relationships (including outsourcing), and technology exchange agreements and licensing. [9]. This classification was chosen, as it describes organisational interdependency and was expected to impact roadmapping.

Joint R&D partnerships are formed by two or more companies that share some of their activities, but still remain independent. Joint R&D partnerships include both joint ventures and joint development agreements. Joint ventures are created by partners, who agree to combine their skills and resources in a separate company characterised by joint ownership. In the joint development agreements, companies pool their resources with the aim of organising the joint R&D activities of two or more companies. On the other hand, customer-supplier relationships are close contacts between customers and suppliers. Generally, the customer is the purchasing organisation of the software product or service and the supplier is the provider of the software or service to the customer. A common form of customer-supplier relationship is called outsourcing, which means subcontracting a process to a third party company. According to Wikipedia [10] *"Outsourcing involves contracting with a supplier, which may or may not involve some degree of offshoring. Offshoring is the transfer of an organisational function to another country, regardless of whether the work is outsourced or stays within the same corporation/company."* In this paper, outsourcing is seen as a part of customer-supplier relationship collaboration mode, thus outsourcing is not discussed separately. Furthermore, technology exchange means the exchange of knowledge, technology or information between two or more companies. The technology exchange agreements cover technology sharing agreements, cross-licensing and the mutual second-sourcing of existing technologies. The licensing means that a company is granted the right to use a specific patented technology in return for a payment. [2, 9, 11]

3 Research Design

The research was carried out as a case study research, which is an empirical inquiry that investigates a phenomenon within its real-life context [12]. The empirical data was collected through questionnaire studies and interviews. These data collection methods were chosen, as the aim of the study was to find out important activities in collaborative product roadmapping and the challenges that inter-company collaboration sets for the product roadmapping process based on companies' experiences. In this section, the data collection and analysis methods used are introduced and the background of the respondents is presented.

3.1 Data Collection and Analysis

The empirical study was carried out in four phases: 1) a questionnaire, 2) analysis of the questionnaire results, 3) interviews, and 4) the analysis of findings. The data collection was carried out in the form of questionnaires and interviews. This paper focuses on the results from the interviews because they give more detailed knowledge on product roadmapping in inter-company collaboration. The purpose of the questionnaire was to form the interview questions and focus the interviews on the important issues in product roadmapping. The questionnaire was also used in selecting the interviewees. The role of the questionnaire and the questions are described in more detail in [8].

First, available literature was examined to gain overall knowledge of state-of-the-art product roadmapping, and to prepare the questionnaire. After that, a produced survey questionnaire was sent to potentially interested contacts, i.e. companies assumed to have experience with product roadmapping, through VTT's[2] [13] electronic mailing lists. The questionnaire was also sent to all the partners of the Merlin project. Thus, the survey was e-mailed to over 600 respondents in the summer of 2006. The response rate of the questionnaire was quite low, being only 9.8 %. However, the 52 replies from 34 different companies formed a good basis for further analysis. The companies who chose to take part in this survey came from Finland, Sweden and the Netherlands.

After the questionnaire studies, work continued with interviews in order to find in detail, how different collaboration modes affect the product roadmapping. In the questionnaire, the respondents were asked whether they would be interested in participating in further research in the form of an interview. Seventeen of the respondents replied that they would be willing to participate in an interview. Because of time limits, not all of the respondents could be interviewed, instead, the interviewees were selected based on the experience of the respondent in product roadmapping in collaboration.

Altogether, nine persons from eight different companies were questioned via both phone and face-to-face interviews. The interviews were semi-structured, since the interviews included both structured and unstructured questions, and proceeded along certain vital themes of the research [14]. The vital themes of the research were created, based on literature analysis and findings of the questionnaire studies. The themes were the same for all of the interviewees, however the questions varied between the different interview sessions based on interviewee's expertise. All of the interviews were audio recorded, so that the responses could be verified after the interview in order to gain the correct information.

The qualitative data was analysed by using a generic process of data analysis presented by Creswell [15]. Thus, after the interviews, the audio recordings were transcribed. Thereafter, all of the data was read through in order to obtain a general sense of the data. Then, a coding process was used to categorise the data and to label the categories. The purpose of the coding process was also to generate a description of the categories, to generate a small number of themes that appeared as major findings of the qualitative data. The description and themes were then presented in qualitative narrative, and finally, an interpretation of the data was made.

---

[2] VTT (Valtion Teknillinen Tutkimuskeskus) Technical Research Centre of Finland the biggest multitechnological applied research organisation in Northern Europe.
URL: http://www.vtt.fi/?lang=en

3.2 Background of the Respondents

Of the total of 52 questionnaire respondents, 33 respondents had experience in product roadmapping in collaboration. Most of the respondents had experience of more than one mode of collaboration. The following table (Table 1) describes the background experiences of the questionnaire respondents.

Table 1. Product roadmapping experiences of questionnaire respondents

Experience on Product Roadmapping			
Total number of respondents	Experiences in product roadmapping **in collaboration**	**#**	Experiences in **collaboration** **modes**
52	33	29	Customer-supplier relationships
		15	Joint R & D partnerships
		6	Technology exchange and licensing agreements
	19: No experiences in collaborative product roadmapping.		

Based on the experiences of questionnaire respondents in different collaboration modes, nine persons were selected for detailed interviews. Of the nine interviewees, seven persons had experience in customer-supplier relationships, five persons had experience in joint R&D partnerships, and two persons had experience in technology exchange and licensing agreements. Hence, mostly information relating to customer-supplier relationships was gained.

The demographic data of the interviewees is presented in Table 2, indicating the nationality of the company, the company size, and the role of the interviewee.

Table 2. Demographic data of the interviewees

Interviewee	Nationality of the company	Company size *	Role of the interviewee
1	Finnish	> 250 employees	Manager
2	Finnish	> 250 employees	Group Manager
3	Finnish	50–250 employees	Chief Technology Officer
4	Finnish	> 250 employees	Product Designer
5	Finnish	< 10 employees	Program Director
6	Finnish	> 250 employees	Group Manager
7	Finnish	> 250 employees	Chief Engineer
8	Swedish	> 250 employees	Senior Researcher
9	Finnish	50–250 employees	Manager

In this paper, only the results from the interviews are presented. The questionnaire replies form the base for the interviews, as the interviewees were selected based on the questionnaire study and the experience of the interviewees on product roadmapping in collaboration. In addition, the details of the interview questions were adjusted based on the questionnaire results, e.g., the details were asked for challenges that were the most important according to the questionnaire results. Detailed results of the questionnaire and the interviews are documented in [8]. In following section, results from the interviews are presented in summary.

4 Empirical Findings

In this section, the results of the interview studies are presented. First, the industrial experiences of product roadmapping in inter-company collaboration are introduced and the main benefits of the process are presented. Then, important issues in collaborative product roadmapping are described. After that, creating product roadmaps in inter-company collaboration is illustrated, and product roadmapping reflecting to collaboration modes is clarified. At the end of the section, the collaboration effects on product roadmapping are identified. Finally, the validity and limitations of the study are discussed.

All interviewees perceive a roadmap as a plan, a leading map, of the company's future directions. A product roadmap also helps to structure and arrange the product development, in order to know how to use certain resources and what is to be done and when. A product roadmap also provides a high-level understanding of scoping the strategy, which allows better planning and commitment to the set plans. Many of the interviewees also pointed out that product roadmapping improves predictability, and hence reduces the occurrence of surprises during the development. A product roadmap was also seen as a central method for communication, as it gives a clear idea on what is about to be done and enables communication in regards to forthcoming strategic projects.

In a collaboration situation, a good roadmap is the main document describing what the parties have agreed and what is about to be done together, so everybody knows the goals. On a good roadmap, it can be seen what others are currently doing and in which phase they should be in. Thus, a roadmap simplifies the synchronisation between collaboration parties and also provides vigour, backbone and predictability of product development for the partners.'

4.1 Important Issues in Collaborative Product Roadmapping

Co-operation in different layers of product development, for instance with component manufacturers, regulators, standardisation organisations, and end-customers, was found to be always important among the interviewees. The reason was that more perspectives would be involved in the product roadmapping and thus the content of the roadmap could be more precise. An interviewee, who had experience in customer-supplier relationships, pointed out: *"There has to be a customer need or an actual customership to confirm the goal of the roadmap. Thus, the customer also acts as a controller for the product proposal that the roadmap stays on track and that something useful is being created."* Co-operation was hence viewed as important and without actual collaboration partner involvement, the roadmap could not have been successful.

Project management was also thought to be always essential, especially when multiple actors were involved in the roadmapping process. This was since problems were caused when tasks were divided between partners, as nobody wanted to do more than their own part. Additionally, traditional roles between partners were found to be often vital, especially, during prioritising features in order to know who makes the final decision about the priorities. Thus, those persons who had the ability and powers to also say that this is vital and this should be done first had to be involved in the roadmapping process.

Openness between the partners in order to mutually share ideas and views was also seen as often important, since it was essential to understand each other's views and reasons. Anyhow, knowledge had to be shared without loosing critical confidentiality. Hence, the creation of good and confidential relationships with all customer and co-operation partners was significant. Moreover, creating long lasting customer relationships and, thereby, creating a reliable image of the case company to the customer was found to be essential.

Based on most of the interviewees, *the partners had to participate closely* in the product roadmapping process. Since if partners prepared for the product implementation in the wrong way, then the required products might not have been created. Thus, the partner had to have components, production lines, and test arrangements with the correct features, in order to create the right products. Furthermore, determining the IPRs of the product was important, particularly when something new was being created.

Continuous communication with collaboration partners was always important as well, since there were several changes during the process. Daily communication between the collaboration partners was arranged through regular meetings, phone calls, and email. At the beginning of the roadmapping process, face-to-face meetings were thought to be particularly important in order to avoid misunderstandings. Thereafter, participation in regular follow-up meetings was vital, in order to keep track of the product development. The partners could also come together ad hoc, in the case of major changes to the product. Communication was also arranged through boards and forums, as well as exchanging documents between partners.

4.2 Creating Product Roadmaps in Inter-company Collaboration

The creation of the product roadmap in inter-company collaboration depended on the product to be developed and the form of co-operation, as presented in Figure 2. For instance, product roadmapping in collaboration was affected by the following aspects: the period of the product's life-span, the closeness of the relationships, and the type of partnership, i.e. who was in control of the activities taking place.

When co-operation was long and tight, the product roadmaps were created together. For example, when the product was being created for the client, the partner then became part of the client company, and thus the co-operation became very close. Thus, inter-company collaboration between subcontracting partners can be considered to be tight. Additionally, in the case of products with long life spans, product roadmaps were created in closer co-operation and the companies' roadmaps were shared more mutually. That was partly because partners wanted to correspond to each other's future challenges. Instead, in loose co-operation situations, when the partnership was not so long lasting and intensive, or the purpose was to create a short

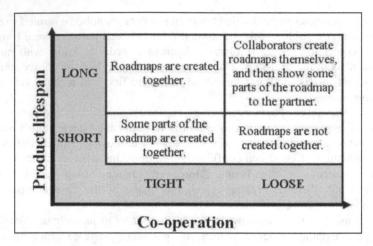

Fig. 2. Creating product roadmaps in inter-company collaboration

life span product, the partners didn't then create the product roadmaps together. In that case, the partners created the roadmaps by themselves and then shared or showed some parts of the roadmap to the partner. Furthermore, this was the case when the customer was a competitor.

According to most of the interviewees, product roadmaps were created together with collaboration partners through negotiations. Information was shared between the partners, and if there were any misalignments, then they had to be solved, so there was always conciliation involved. Additionally, tools which allow the collection and sorting out of the received feedback were used in the creation of the product roadmaps. In one case, when most of the product was created together with collaboration partners, the product roadmapping process took the practices of the partners into account early on. Therefore, before launching the actual project, the negotiations were conducted and the contracts were signed between the collaboration partners. In the contracts, contact persons from both partners were agreed upon and the creation of the product roadmaps was defined. In addition, the means of steering the roadmap creation process, e.g. regular project meetings, were defined in the contracts. The contracts could also include obligations of the partners to inform the other if they acquire new technology that affects the content of the roadmap.

Moreover, when the product roadmaps were created together with collaboration partners, it was important to write down unambiguous and clear features that could be set on a timeline. The timeline presented when the features were to be ready and what their quality was. This ensured that all relevant parties had a mutual understanding of the features and the whole product. It was also important to approve the milestones together and to synchronise the processes, when there were more collaborators involved in the process. Therefore, the product roadmapping process required more brainstorming and going through the ideas jointly.

When product roadmaps were created together with collaboration partners, it produced results that were more accurate than when product roadmaps were created inside the company. This was because mutual interests were then aligned through communication. Collaboration also saved on processing time and enabled better visibility, common understanding, as well as the efficient use of resources.

4.3 Product Roadmapping Reflecting to Collaboration Modes

In a *customer-supplier relationship*, such as outsourcing, product roadmapping begins with planning, sharing information, and communication to create a mutual vision of the product. Thus, a central idea in creating product roadmaps together with the customer and supplier was to create a mutual understanding before the product was implemented. However, the roadmap was often seen as a business secret and competitive advantage and therefore, confidentiality was important in the customer-supplier relationships.

The interviewees had several views on how the roadmaps were created in the customer-supplier relationship. For instance, according to one group of interviewees, the company only had specific points in time when they met with their partners, which was not on a daily basis. So, in practice, the partners did not create the product roadmaps together, but the partners' viewpoints were collected as input into the roadmaps. The created roadmaps were then shown to the partners to the appropriate extent; meaning that not all of the confidential information was shown. On the other hand, according to another interviewee group, customers (e.g., outsourcers or client organisations) and suppliers (e.g., vendors or subcontractors) participated in the creation of the product roadmaps. Particularly, the customers were present, since they were regarded as the dominant partners, whose opinion ruled. In addition, when the product was being developed together with a subcontractor and there was a common customer, the customer made the final decisions.

When the product roadmap was created in *joint R&D partnerships*, then the partners had to have a mutual understanding of each other's roadmaps and deeper insights into them. Additionally, the partners had to be able to disclose confidential matters. In this kind of relationship, one was the leading partner, who had the overall idea of the product to be developed. The other partner supported and provided input into the process. The leading partner created the first idea of the product, and was most likely the owner of the roadmap. However, the supporting partner was also closely involved in creating the idea of the product and in other phases as well, particularly the parts that affected them. The supporting partner also helped the leading partner to create the roadmap and the final view of the product.

When the product roadmaps were created together with *technology exchange or licensing agreement* partners, the relationship was then more a matter of legal agreements and contracts that controlled the strategy. Therefore, according to one group of interviewees, it was not as common to share roadmaps as in the other modes of collaboration. Thus, the technology exchange and licensing agreements were more a matter of disclosure and trust. The partners had their own roadmaps, and there was an agreement on a strategy. This meant that the partners only showed the schedule requirements to each other, and not the actual roadmaps. However, according to another interviewee group, when a part of the product was created by a partner, e.g. a commercial off-the-shelf (COTS) vendor, then the roadmap was partly created together. This was because the vendor could then declare whether the desired features could be done in a certain way or within a given schedule. The vendor could also bring out matters that affected the whole roadmap, e.g. matters that the integrator did not realise or did not notice before.

The differences between the three collaboration modes are presented in Table 3.

Table 3. Differences between collaboration modes

Collaboration Mode	Important activities	Product Roadmapping
Customer-supplier relationship (incl. outsourcing)	– Mutual vision of the product – Mutual understanding – Confidentiality and secrecy	1. Roadmaps were not created together, but the partners' viewpoints were collected as input into the roadmaps. The roadmaps were shown to the partners to some extent. 2. Roadmaps were created together. The customer made the final decisions.
Joint R&D partnership	– Mutual understanding of each other's roadmaps – Disclose confidential matters	1. Roadmaps were created together.
Technology exchange or licensing agreement	– Legal agreements and contracts	1. The partners had their own roadmaps, and there was an agreement on a line strategy, e.g. the partners only showed the schedule requirements to each other, and not the actual roadmaps. 2. In a COTS vendor case, the roadmap was partly created together. The vendor declared whether the desired features could be done in a certain way or within a given schedule.

4.4 Collaboration Effects to Product Roadmapping

Product roadmapping in inter-company collaboration is a complex and multi-dimensional process. Empirical findings indicate that collaboration effects each phase of the product roadmapping process differently. These effects are not divided based on the collaboration types, but discussed in general. The effects are summarised in Table 4.

Collaboration had effects in capturing features, since the partners could provide suggestions, boundary conditions, and limitations for creating the roadmaps. Also, when features were captured together with the partners, it enabled the efficient use of resources, since there was the possibility to stimulate and analyse various approaches.

Partners usually participated in the analysis to suggest their own opinions on the features. One of the interviewees replied *"Collaboration affects feature analysis, since it helps to verify things faster"*. There could be disagreements and misunderstanding between partners during the analysis, as one of the interviewees explained: *"Some features are more important to the partner, and it causes some other features to be left outside the product, so compromises have to be made."*

Table 4. Summary of collaboration effects to product roadmapping

Phase	Effect of Collaboration
Capturing Features	– Suggestions, boundary conditions and limitations given by the partner – Efficient use of resources
Analysing Features	– Help to verify features faster – Disagreements and misunderstanding between partners – Partners value different features, so compromises have to be made – Partners participate in the analysis to suggest their opinions – Continuous communication required
Prioritising Features	– More information is available for decision-making – Prioritisation is more complex – Important to create mutual understanding
Roadmap Validation and Agreement	– More information is available for decision-making – Improves the roadmap's business relevance – More complicated to reach agreements – Partners have to be committed – Makes the roadmap a legal agreement
Change Management of the Roadmap	– Regular co-operation and meetings with the customers and partners to notice a change proposal and to review the roadmaps – Clear roles between the collaborators to divide change management tasks – Changes to the roadmap also mean changes to the co-operation agreement

Continuous communication with the partner was also needed, since during analysis, missing features, for instance, were noticed.

According to most of the interviewees, collaboration aided prioritisation, as more information was faster and easier available for decision-making. On the other hand, prioritisation was also considered to be more complex by some of the interviewees, since more stakeholders were involved.

Collaboration also affected roadmap validation and agreement. As one of the interviewees described, *"More information is then available for decision-making"*. Another interviewee noted, *"Collaboration improves the business relevance of the roadmap, as more perspectives are involved, but then it is also more complicated to reach an agreement."* Additionally, the partners had to be committed to the roadmap and the product development. Therefore, the roadmap was typically a legal agreement, which had to be updated when changes occurred.

Regular co-operation and meetings with the customers and partners were seen as important, because the change proposal was then commonly noticed and the roadmaps were reviewed. In order to divide the change management tasks, the roles between the collaborators had to be clear. For instance, in the customer-supplier agreement, when the customer proposed a change, e.g. a change in the customer's technical environment or in a feature's priority order, then the customer was in change of analysing and approving the change. When collaborators were involved in the roadmapping, changes to the roadmap also then meant changes to the co-operation agreement. Furthermore, if the change request affected the partner, then the partner had to be involved in the change management process as well. In that case, the partner's reply was included in the impact analysis, and the input from the partner's change impact analysis was taken into the change management process.

4.5 Validity and Limitations of the Study

The data in this study can be considered to be adequate as altogether 52 applicable questionnaire replies were received and nine persons in total were interviewed. Furthermore, the questionnaire responses came from altogether 34 different companies. Additionally, similarities could clearly be seen among the replies, hence the sampling can be considered as adequate. However, it should be noted that most of the respondents were Finnish, although the replies between different nationalities didn't diverge largely from each other. The respondents also have subjective perspectives to the issues asked, thus the answers do not reveal the whole opinion of the company, only the opinions of the respondent. Additionally, most of the case companies were considered as large organisations with more than 250 employees, thus the results may not be directly applicable to smaller companies. In addition, the research results apply to companies that are involved in software products or service development.

5 Discussion and Conclusions

A product roadmap provides a clear focus towards product development, and provides a high-level understanding for scoping the strategy. On the other hand, a clear strategy allows a better planning and commitment to the set plans. Product roadmapping also improves predictability, and hence reduces surprises during the development.

Based on literature, the main challenges caused by inter-company collaboration can be derived from planning activities in product roadmapping, because at that point customisation issues are taken into account, and business and process objectives are articulated [16, 17]. Furthermore, communication between partners, a degree of trust, ownership of the roadmap, nominated persons, and a common language gained by training, are the main challenge during the product roadmapping process [5, 16, 18, 19].

The empirical results revealed that continuous communication is important and, especially, at the beginning of the product roadmapping process, face-to-face meetings are essential to avoid misunderstandings. In order to mutually share ideas and views, openness between collaboration partners is important. However, knowledge should be shared without loosing critical confidentiality. Hence, creating good and confidential relationships with partners, as well as creating long lasting customer relationships, are of high importance. In contrary to literature, the empirical findings draw attention to determining the product's property rights, particularly when something new is being created. Sharing the intellectual property rights between the collaboration partners should be defined clearly. The empirical results highlighted that collaboration in different layers of the product development is essential in order to gain more perspectives to the product roadmapping process. Project management is also challenging in a collaboration situation, because in the case of multiple actors in the product roadmapping process, problems are caused during dividing tasks between partners, as duplicate work and grey areas should be avoided.

The empirical results revealed that creating a product roadmap in inter-company collaboration depends on the product to be developed and the form of co-operation. Product roadmapping in inter-company collaboration is affected by the following aspects: the period of the product's life span, the closeness of the relationships, and the type of the partnership, i.e. who is in control of the activities taking place. In a customer-supplier relationship, such as outsourcing, the central idea in creating product roadmaps together is to create a mutual understanding and ensure the confidentiality of the roadmap. In joint R&D partnerships, confidentiality was seen as important. However, the major difference compared to the customer-supplier relationship was that either one of the joint R&D partners is the leading partner, who had the overall idea of the product to be developed and most likely was the owner of the roadmap. In technology exchange or licensing agreements, the relationship was considered as more of a matter of legal agreements and contracts, and thus the roadmaps were not shared so freely as in the other collaboration modes. Empirical findings also indicate that collaboration affects to each phase of the product roadmapping process differently.

This paper provided an empirical understanding and experiences about product roadmapping, which has not been previously systematically explored. The research results point out important activities in collaborative product roadmapping and challenges that collaboration sets for the product roadmapping process. The findings describe how product roadmaps are created in inter-company collaboration and how product roadmapping reflects on different collaboration modes. These research results increase product roadmapping knowledge that can help companies to improve their own product roadmapping processes, by taking into account the most challenging and important activities of product roadmapping in collaboration.

Acknowledgements

This paper has been written within the Merlin project, which is an ITEA project. The authors would like to thank the support of ITEA [20] and Tekes [21].

References

1. Phaal, R., Farrukh, C., Probert, D.: Developing a Technology Roadmapping System. In: Technology Management: A Unifying Discipline for Melting the Boundaries, pp. 99–111 (2005)
2. Hagedoorn, J.: Inter-Firm R&D Partnerships - an Overview of Major Trends and Patterns since 1960. Research Policy 31, 477–492 (2002)
3. McMillian, A.: Roadmapping - Agent of Change. Res. Technol. Manage. 46, 40–47 (2003)
4. Albright, R.E.: A Unifying Architecture for Roadmaps Frames a Value Scorecard. In: Proceedings of the IEEE International Engineering Management Conference, pp. 383–386 (2003)
5. Albright, R.E., Kappel, T.A.: Roadmapping in the Corporation. Res. Technol. Manage. 46, 31–40 (2003)

6. Lehtola, L., Kauppinen, M., Kujala, S.: Linking the Business View to Requirements Engineering: Long-Term Product Planning by Roadmapping. In: Proceedings of the 13th IEEE International Conference on Requirements Engineering (RE 2005), pp. 439–446 (2005)
7. Tabrizi, B., Walleigh, R.: Defining Next-Generation Products: An Inside Look. Harv. Bus. Rev. 75, 116–124 (1997)
8. Kynkäänniemi, T.: Product roadmapping in collaboration. VTT Publications 625, Espoo (2007)
9. Duysters, G., Hagedoorn, J.: A Note on Organizational Modes of Strategic Technology Partnering. Journal of Scientific & Industrial Research 58, 640–649 (2000)
10. Wikipedia, http://en.wikipedia.org/wiki/Outsourcing
11. Hagedoorn, J.: Understanding the Rationale of Strategic Technology Partnering: Interorganizational Modes of Cooperation and Sectoral Differences. Strategic Manage. J. 14, 371–385 (1993)
12. Yin, R.K.: Applied social research methods series vol. 5; case study research: Design and methods, 2nd edn. Sage Publications, Inc., Thousand Oaks (1994)
13. VTT, Technical Research Centre of Finland, http://www.vtt.fi/?lang=en
14. Järvinen, P.: On research methods. Opinpajan kirja, Tampere, Finland (2001)
15. Creswell, J.W.: Research design: Qualitative, quantitative, and mixed method approaches, 2nd edn. Sage Publications, Thousand Oaks (2003)
16. Phaal, R., Farrukh, C., Probert, D.: Technology Roadmapping: Linking Technology Resources to Business Objectives. In: Proceedings of the 4th International Conference on Management Innovative Manufacturing, (MIMZOOO) (2000)
17. Phaal, R., Farrukh, C., Mills, J., Probert, D.: Customizing the Technology Roadmapping Approach. In: Proceedings of the Portland International Conference on Management of Engineering and Technology (PICMET), pp. 361–369 (2003)
18. Groenveld, P.: Roadmapping Integrates Business and Technology. Res. Technol. Manage. 40, 48–55 (1997)
19. Phaal, R., Farrukh, C., Probert, D.: Fast-Start Technology Roadmapping. In: Proceedings of the 9th International Conference on Management of Technology (IAMOT), pp. 1–12 (2000)
20. ITEA, Information Technology for European Advancement, http://www.itea-office.org/
21. Tekes, Finnish Funding Agency for Technology and Innovation, http://www.tekes.fi/eng/

Global Software Development with Cloud Platforms

Pavan Yara, Ramaseshan Ramachandran, Gayathri Balasubramanian,
Karthik Muthuswamy, and Divya Chandrasekar

Cognizant Technology Solutions,
5/639 Old Mahabalipuram Road, Kandanchavadi, Chennai - 600096, India
{Pavankumar.Yara,Ramaseshan.Ramachandran,Gayathri.Balasubramanian,
Karthik.Muthuswamy,Divya.Chandrasekar}@cognizant.com
http://www.cognizant.com/

Abstract. Offshore and outsourced distributed software development
models and processes are facing challenges, previously unknown, with
respect to computing capacity, bandwidth, storage, security, complexity,
reliability, and business uncertainty. Clouds promise to address these
challenges by adopting recent advances in virtualization, parallel and
distributed systems, utility computing, and software services. In this
paper, we envision a cloud-based platform that addresses some of these
core problems. We outline a generic cloud architecture, its design and our
first implementation results for three cloud forms - a compute cloud, a
storage cloud and a cloud-based software service- in the context of global
distributed software development (GSD). Our "compute cloud"provides
computational services such as continuous code integration and a compile
server farm, "storage cloud" offers storage (block or file-based) services
with an on-line virtual storage service, whereas the on-line virtual labs
represent a useful cloud service. We note some of the use cases for clouds
in GSD, the lessons learned with our prototypes and identify challenges
that must be conquered before realizing the full business benefits. We
believe that in the future, software practitioners will focus more on these
cloud computing platforms and see clouds as a means to supporting a
ecosystem of clients, developers and other key stakeholders.

Keywords: Globally Distributed Software Development, Cloud computing, Software-as-a-Service, compute cloud, storage cloud.

1 Introduction

The last decade has witnessed Globally Distributed Software Development(GSD)
model becoming a business necessity to capitalize on global resource pools,
attractive cost structures, and round-the-clock development for achieving faster
cycle-time accelerations [3,26,31]. At the same time, GSD has also brought
unique nuances, complexities, and challenges ranging from *technical*, *temporal*,
spatial, and *process* standpoints [4,25,34]. Some of these issues are long standing
such as effective capacity planning, resource provisioning, software lifecycle

O. Gotel, M. Joseph, and B. Meyer (Eds.): SEAFOOD 2009, LNBIP 35, pp. 81–95, 2009.

management, communication, coordination, and collaboration mechanisms. In addition, we are also seeing relatively new challenges with the rise of *multi cores, virtualization*, recent *programming frameworks & abstractions*, and other complex advances. Now, with the intensification of global economic activity and the resulting demand for cost/benefit analysis, the need for better outsourcing software engineering and management approaches has only become more pronounced. Also, over the years, the various structured and other disciplined software engineering approaches, advocated as key remedies for addressing these GSD challenges, have undergone refinement. A range of new, effective platforms and practices have emerged and have been adopted to address these unique challenges of GSD. These mechanisms - such as better communication and coordination practices [7], management of global software teams [28], effective resource leveraging with virtual teams [33], collaboration and knowledge management tools & techniques [16], programming methodologies and processes [13], software lifecycle models, service oriented architecture [27] concepts specifically web services and web 2.0 technologies, grid infrastructures to provide IT services [17] - have succesfully tried to address the GSD challenges.

In this paper, we discuss one such emerging paradigm with several possible positive implications for GSD. "Cloud computing", as it is popularly known, is a paradigm that represents a *disruptive* business and technology concept with different meanings for different GSD ecosystem partners. For example, for IT users, it is a way to deliver computing, storage and applications over the network, often the Internet, from centralized data centers. For application developers, it is an internet-scale software development platform and run-time environment with several interesting use case scenarios such as always-on and always-available development environments, content collaboration spaces to share code, documents, presentations, discussions in a Facebook mode social media style, and services like online IDEs, continuous code builds and testing. For infrastructure providers and administrators, it is a massive, distributed data center infrastructure connected by IP networks to achieve economies of scale and grant "on-demand" access to computing capacity. Thus, cloud computing delivers "IT" as a service (ITaaS) which can be adapted to address some of the core challenges in the GSD.

Cloud computing tries to replace the traditional *desktop-as-a-platform* with *network-as-a-platform* model. As such, it builds on decades of research in virtualization, parallel and distributed systems, utility computing, and more recent advances in the fields of networking, Web, and software services. The key idea of this paradigm is to provide a *utility service*, similar to a power grid, into which a user may plug-in regardless of location to access always-on, always-available, and device-independent IT services. In this way, it represents the next natural step in the evolution of computing and IT services. It promises to maximize the productivity of all IT-related activities. One such instance is where time and resources spent building or customizing application frameworks or building software/hardware infrastructure could be better spent on improving the business logic with cloud paradigm.

We explore the nature and potential of clouds in the paper. The main contribution of this paper is in laying a cloud-based vision for GSD and formulating a generic architecture to address some of the GSD challenges. In doing so, we also showcase how we realize key business benefits with our cloud-based platforms. Our cloud platforms are easily adaptable to provide a common, managed, and powerful infrastructure to support GSD activities. Accordingly, the paper is structured as follows: we explain the basic concepts underlying cloud computing paradigm in Section 2 and discuss how clouds can be used within GSD ecosystem in Section 3. As such, we present a preliminary architecture of the framework and discuss candidate technologies to realize it in Section 4. Section 5 describes three GSD adaptable cloud service prototypes done at our lab - a *Compute cloud* providing computational services such as continuous code builds and integration with on-demand infrastructure; a *Storage cloud* providing massive online storage for software project-related artifacts, and a cloud-based online virtual lab solution for providing always-on and always-available training, testing and debugging facilities - before concluding.

2   Cloud Computing Paradigm

Cloud Computing fulfills the long held dream of computing as a utility [45] and thus has the potential to transform how the IT ecosystem makes and uses hardware and software as a *utility* and a *service*.

2.1   Concepts

The term *Cloud Computing* usually refers to online delivery and consumption model for business and customer services. These include IT services like *Software-as-a-Service (SaaS)* and *Storage or Server capacity as a service* and many non-IT business and consumer services which are not computing tasks. All these are commonly referred to as *X-as-a-Service (XaaS)*. However, for our paper, we adopt these following definitions:

Cloud is a pool of highly scalable, abstracted infrastructure, capable of hosting end-customer applications, that is billed by consumption [20].

Cloud services refer to the consumer and business products, services and solutions that are delivered and consumed in real-time over network.

Cloud Computing is an emerging IT development, deployment and delivery model which enables real-time delivery of products, services, and solutions over the Web (i.e., enabling cloud services).

Technically, this paradigm refers to providing services on virtual machines allocated on top of a large machine pool, whereas in business terms, the term means a method to address scalability and availability concerns for applications.

2.2 Characteristics

From an higher abstraction point, three aspects are primary to clouds - *Elasticity*, *Pay-per-use model*, and *High-Availability*. The key characteristics of cloud services, in the lines of Forrester [20], are as follows:

1. *Standardized IT-based capability:* Delivers compute, storage, network or software-based capabilities, solely or in combination through standard offerings.
2. *Accessible via Internet protocols from any computer:* Standards-based, universal network access through a regular web browser via HTTP, XMPP, Open ID, OAuth or Atom protocols.
3. *Always available*, and *scales automatically to adjust to demand:* Resilient and highly available; elastic enough to cope with scale and demand.
4. *Pay-per-use or advertising-based:* Service is paid up in three ways - advertising, subscription or transaction based.
5. *Web or programmatic-based control interfaces:* Uses service-based interfaces like XML, JSON and REST-style software connection standards.
6. *Offers full customer self-service:* Customers can provision, manage, and terminate services themselves and the control is via a Web interface or programmatic call to service APIs.

2.3 Examples

Although the paradigm has emerged only recently, the implications of IT services provided through it are wide-reaching [5,8,40,45]. Cloudy infrastructure companies such as Amazon and GoGrid offer data storage priced by the gigabyte per month and computing capacity by the CPU-hour [1]. **Office and productivity applications** such as Google Apps [21], Zoho office suite, MS SharePoint Online, Cisco WebEx in the cloud make collaboration more accessible and highly available. **SaaS** companies offer *CRM services* through their multi-tenant shared facilities so that clients can manage their customers without buying software [39]. These use cases represent only the beginning of options for delivering all kinds of complex capabilities like online businesses, collaboration tools, R&D projects, quick project promotions, partner integration, new business ventures [11,40], etc.

2.4 Benefits

The economic appeal of clouds is often summed up by the statement *converting capital expenses to operating expenses* [2]. There are other clear business benefits such as almost zero upfront infrastructure investment, just-in-time infrastructure, more efficient resource utilization, usage-based costing and a real potential for shrinking the processing time. We recommend the reader to refer [2,5,8,11,36,40] for more details.

2.5   Public, Private and Hybrid Clouds

As discussed in the introduction, clouds are the result of the natural transformation of the IT infrastructure of enterprises over the last decade and can take many forms and can be of many types. In this paper, we look at three major types of clouds.

Public clouds are cloud services offered by third-party providers (vendors) such as Amazon, Google, Salesforce.com for public consumption. The vendors fully host and manage the infrastructure and charge customers for the resources they use, usually on a hourly or transaction based interaction. *Private clouds* are cloud services provided within the enterprise firewall and managed by the enterprises such as Boeing or GM. They offer the same benefits as public clouds but with fine-grained control, security and compliance norms. The major difficulty with private clouds is the complexity and cost involved in setting up "internal" clouds. *Hybrid Clouds* are a combination of public and private cloud properties. They leverage services that are in both the public and private work spaces and are typically used in scenarios like where they need to receive customer payments or do employee payroll processing. The major drawback with hybrid clouds is the difficulty in effectively creating and governing such a solution [18].

3   Cloud Platforms for GSD

While we are yet to see fundamentally new types of applications enabled by cloud computing, we believe that it offers compelling benefits with several important classes of existing applications for GSD model. The cloud paradigm, by its design, tries to optimize IT-related productivity by taking care of scaling and availability concerns and redirecting resources to long term strategic business development. Emphasizing communication, collaborative work and community interaction, we perceive clouds to offer huge leverage in many of the GSD related activities. For example, when companies outsource tasks, those tasks often require close working relationships between the companies involved. These collaborations grow organically to form communities around the particular task they aim to solve. This presents multiple issues. In previous generations of GSD, the environments and tools had to be made available to teams involved; organizations had to acquire the tools at their own cost, pool resources to provision the requested job; workers couldn't locate and use their best tools for the job as determined by them; and they had to span time and space to share, discuss, collaborate or even publish content where necessary, as time and circumstance required. In addition, the exchange of content that happens in multiple forms such as emails, discussion forums, bug tracking systems, version control systems and logging, make it a very complex activity. Cloud-based platforms can be used for such cases, in the form of content collaboration spaces and always-on and always-accessible IT services. In this section, we discuss three such useful areas for GSD - *development, quality assurance & testing, and IT operations*.

3.1   Development

Clouds offer instant resource provisioning, flexibility, on-the-fly scaling, and high-availability for continuously evolving GSD-related activities. Some of the use cases include:

- **Development Environments:** With clouds, the ability to acquire, deploy, configure, and host development environments becomes "on-demand". The development environments are, then, always-on and always-available to the concerned teams with fine-grained access control mechanisms. In addition, the development environments can be purpose-built with support for application-level tools, source code repositories, and programming tools. After the project is done, these can also be archived or destroyed. The other key element of these "on-demand" hosting environments is the flexibility through its quick "prototyping" support. Prototyping becomes flexible, in that as new code and ideas can be quickly turned into workable Proof-Of-Concepts and tested.
- **Developer Tools:** Hosting developer tools such as IDEs and simple code editors in the cloud eliminates the need for developers to have local IDEs and other associated development tools. This also offers the concerned project members to access the development environment and tools, across time-zones and places.
- **Content Collaboration Spaces:** Clouds make collaboration and coordination practical, intuitive, and flexible through easy enabling of content collaboration spaces, modeled after the social software domain tools like Facebook or Flickr, but centering on project-related information like invoices, statments, RFPs, requirement docs, documentation, images and data sets. These content spaces can automate many project related tasks such as automatically creating MS Word versions of all imported text documents or as complex as running workflows to collate information from several different organizations working in collaboration. Each content space can be unique, created by composing a set of project requirements. Users can invite internal and external collaborators into this customized environment, assigning appropriate roles and responsibilities. After the group's work is "complete", their content space can be archived or destroyed. These spaces can be designed to support distributed version control systems like *bzr, mercurial,* and *git* enabling social platform conversations and other content management features.
- **Continuous Code Integration:** Compute clouds let **'compile-test-change'** software cycle on-the-fly do continuous builds and integration checks to meet strict quality checks and development guidelines. They can also enforce policies for customized builds.
- **APIs & Programming Frameworks:** Clouds also compel developers to embrace standard programming model APIs where ever possible and adhere to style guides, conventions, and coding standards in meeting the specific project requirements. They also force developers to embrace new programming models and abstractions such as .NET, GWT, Django, Rails,

and Spring for increasing overall productivity. One more key feature of using clouds is that they enforce constraints, which pushes developers to address the critical next-gen programming challenges of multi-cores, parallel programming and virtualization [22].

The software engineering community is also fast evaluating approaches like Agile, Automatic, Extreme, Pair and Re-factoring to suit clouds [2,22]. The above mentioned use cases can be applied within both "public" and "private" clouds. If the client requirements require "security" and "control" to be the main concerns, we recommend offshore development companies to adopt "private" clouds as they allow enterprises to retain control, but at the same time offer them flexibility, availability and economies of scale.

3.2   Testing and Quality Assurance

There are two components to cloud computing in software testing. Clouds provide the computing infrastructure for doing software testing across platforms and in various combinations. The other component uses clouds to run fully functional test cases with industry standard frameworks and regression support. The use of virtual appliances for providing the requested computing requirements is becoming a practice in the software testing domain. Virtual appliances are a set of virtual machines pre-built, pre-configured, ready-to-run applications packaged along with optimized operating systems. These enable flexible and quick software testing. On the other hand, they are also used to automate execution of some industry standard tests, support debugging and code coverage tools to identify gaps in test procedures. In addition, the ability of clouds to simulate thousands of users hitting Web applications is particularly attractive. Thus, *cloudifying* testing services opens up interesting possibilities. One immediate use case is where cloud testing is used to verify the real scalability of sites, servers, applications, and networks in advance of a genuine surge in traffic.

3.3   IT Operations

Now, clouds are increasingly being used to simplify the management part of operations in offshore development centers. Recent studies shows that cloud deployment times can be reduced to less than 6 hours from the traditional IT deployment times of 14-24 days for eight typical IT management tasks [29]. These tasks include operating system tasks like back-up, recovery, installation of patches, network tasks including server assignments, configuration of network and security parameters, installation of software, etc. The first significant advantage of such clouds is the "cost savings" factor. The traditional IT model requires business users to make a front-loaded investment in software and hardware as well as a lifecycle investment in professional staff to maintain servers and upgrade software. Clouds shift much of this expense to a **"pay-as-you-go"** model and so offer significant cost advantages in terms of power, space, cooling, hardware and operations personnel [2,11,24,44]. Other key operations benefits include the ease and effective use for backup and restore activities to provide business continuity; ability to handle security and archiving required for accountability and compliance regulation laws such as SOX, HIPAA and the powerful software configuration management [37] it provides so that infrastructure gets provisioned, deployed and relinquished according to business needs.

4   Our Architecture and Service Offerings

Having listed the cloud advantages for GSD model, we present an applicable and generic high-level architecture of clouds, and a hierarchy of cloud service offerings possible with our architecture to benefit all the key stakeholders in the ecosystem.

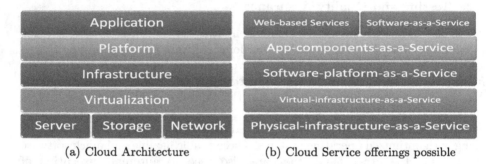

(a) Cloud Architecture   (b) Cloud Service offerings possible

Fig. 1. Generic Cloud Architecture and various service offerings possible with the architecture

4.1   Architecture Overview

We present our architecture as a layered stack to suitably represent the growing list of technologies and IT offerings in this space. There are several elements to the entire GSD ecosystem and the architecture is envisioned as being spread-out over and catering to cover most of these elements (generic and abstract). Figure 1(a) shows a generic cloud architecture for GSD. The *Application layer* covers the Web-based UIs, web service APIs, multi-tenant architecture and a rich variety of configuration options. The *Platform layer* adds a software stack to the underlying infrastructure layer, manages virtual machines and supports the development, integration and run-time execution of cloud application software. The *Infrastructure layer* makes use of the underlying virtual infrastructure so as to economically scale to very high volumes, and preferably do so in a granular fashion. The *Virtualization layer* abstracts the physical resources like servers, storage or network devices and presents equivalent logical resources for consumption to other layers. The architecture is designed to facilitate service offerings that serve to improve processes in GSD. Thus, we attempt to address issues pertaining to cost constraints, hardware/software resource provisioning and collaboration through our generic and high-level architecture.

4.2   Cloud Service Offerings

Embarking on familiar GSD product categories like developer tools, middleware and IT infrastructure tasks, we segment cloud services based on the proposed cloud architecture, as shown in Figure 1(b).

Software-as-a-Service (SaaS) delivers a single application through the browser to thousands of customers using a multi-tenant architecture. For the customer, it means no upfront investment in servers or software licensing; for the provider, with just one app to maintain, costs are low compared to conventional hosting (e.g., Salesforce.com [39]). *App-components-as-a-Service* spans a spectrum from mash ups to third-party APIs. These app components are aimed at offering developers higher-level software modules for combining existing code to create applications (e.g.,Live Mesh API [32]). This should improve efficiency and encourage code reuse in the development process, which is one of the pain areas in GSD. *Software-platform-as-a-service (PaaS)* is an entirely virtualized platform that includes one or more servers, operating systems, and specific applications (e.g.,Google App Engine [22]). *Virtual-Infrastructure-as-a-service* (IaaS) or *Hardware-as-a- service* (HaaS) is the delivery of computer infrastructure as a service. This layer differs from PaaS in that the virtual hardware is provided without a software stack (e.g., Amazon EC2 [1]). There are other offerings also possible such as communication-as-a-service, desktop-as-a-service, database-as-a-service, data-storage-as-a-service, data-as-a-service, data-mining-as-a-service, finance-as-a-service, framework-as-a-service, IDE-as-a-service, integration-as-a-service, and monitoring-as-a-service [11,14,20,36,44].

4.3   Key Enabling Technologies

A lot of enabling technologies contribute to the outlined cloud architecture Here, we identify some state-of-the-art technologies that make clouds practical and possible:

Virtualization   enables clouds to deliver on-demand IT infrastructures through virtual machines (VMs). VMs are created and managed by a Virtual Machine Monitor (VMM), which is the software layer between the operating system and the physical machine. VM-based platforms offer several advantages including better isolation, availability and portability apart from the flexibility and scalability it brings. There is a lot of renewed interest in virtualized platforms these days which is evident by its presence in various forms such as Server, Desktop, Application, Storage and Network coming from industry players like VMware, Citrix, Microsoft, Red Hat, Cisco, and Sun. For more details, the reader is advised to refer [6,38,43].

MapReduce [15] is the dominant programming model used in clouds that provide on-demand computing capacity. Map Reduce assumes that many common programming applications can be coded as processes that manipulate large data sets of <key,value> pairs. The *Map* process maps each <key, value> pair in the data set into a new pair of <key',value'>. The *Reduce* process, then, merges values with the same key. Although this is seemingly simple model, it has been used to support a large number of applications, that manipulate data. Hadoop is an open source implementation of this model [9]. Stream-based parallel programming models, in which a User Defined Function (UDF) is applied to all the data, are also commonly used.

Other programming models modeled after *Google File System* (GFS) and *Big Table* are also common in many cloud forms. GFS refers to a scalable distributed file system for large data-intensive applications [19]. It not only provides fault tolerance while running on inexpensive commodity hardware, but also delivers high aggregate performance to a large number of clients. Data automatically get distributed to nodes at load time, and are processed locally, in parallel with output data written to local disks, forming a single user-accessible volume. Big Table [12] represents a database layer with the key idea of separating organized storage from query storage. It is a distributed storage system for managing structured data that is designed to scale to a very large size. *HDFS* and *HBase* are the open source implementation of these models [9].

Service-Oriented Architecture (SOA) allows for delivery of an integrated and orchestrated suite of functions to an end-user through composition of both loosely and tightly coupled functions, or services - often network-based, following industry standards like WSDL, SOAP and UDDI [10,27].

Some cloud forms also make use of frameworks such as Pig [35], Zookeeper, Hive, Sawzall [23], LINQ [30], Condor [42] to cope up with the complexity, frequent failured nature of commodity hardware like hard drive crashes, network up-downs.

5   Our Experiments

We have used these technologies to implement three GSD adaptable internal cloud prototypes. This section presents our experiments and initial results.

5.1   Compile Server Farm

The traditional modes of compiling large software projects across clusters has always been done using message passing interfaces such as MPI or OpenMP. These interfaces are difficult to code, prone to errors and often time-consuming. Moreover, in GSD environments, there has always been a need for faster compile and build cycles to test, debug and maintain complex software projects across verticals and domains. In such scenarios, lots of projects gets created, compiled, and maintained on a regular basis to suit the business and client requirements. Each of these projects typically constitute thousands of files, which when compiled might take hours or days together to build and deploy. This *change-compile-test* cycle is one of the most time consuming event of a project and it requires huge resources like server class machines, or clusters.

Our first prototype tries to address this common issue using *compute cloud* concepts. We represent a compute cloud as a "nexus of hardware, software and data which provides compute services over network". Our compute cloud is actually a "compute server farm". By using Hadoop and Condor, we managed to speedup the **Change-Compile-Test** cycle of large software projects. Another, key motivation for our compute clouds is to do continuous software code integration. The following algorithm is used for our *"compute server farm"*.

Algorithm 1. Compute Server Farm with Hadoop and Condor

---

1. Client workstations launch jobs
2. Condor dynamically allocates clusters
3. Hadoop-on-Demand starts the MapReduce program on the clusters
4. MapReduce program reads/writes into HDFS
5. When done, the results are either stored in the HDFS and/or returned to the client
6. Condor reclaims nodes

We tested this approach on compiling and building up Eclipse IDE from its Java source code. Condor [42] is used as a batch scheduler to schedule jobs on idle workstations. We have written a Map-Reduce program [15] targeting the hadoop run time environment to automatically split, distribute, store and parallelize the computation using HDFS [9] as a temporary file storage. We used JDepend for analyzing the source dependencies. The results are encouraging with the total compilation taking about 80 minutes with 5 standard desktop workstations, against a standalone job, taking 150 minutes. Our experience with this approach encourages us to believe that this is a viable and simpler way of mimicking the *compute cloud* for larger GSD projects.

5.2   Online Storage Cloud

The key motivation for an online storage cloud is the need for scalable data management platform to support variety of typical use cases in GSD environments. It should support an ecosystem of users and developments growing around project content and fast-changing content related tasks and ideas across domains and requirements. Additionally, GSD projects have to deal with massive, structured, unstructured and queued files. This sheer number of files implies cumbersome storage and organization on existing storage systems; for example, while a SAN can provide enough storage, the simple file system interface layered on top of a SAN is not expressive enough to manage these files.

Moreover in such projects, teams and project members tend to move from one location to other based on various business and administrative needs. When such team or project transfers happen, there is a strong demand for personal data backup and restoration requests from all over the project. This presents multiple problems. First, personal computer disks are limited in capacity and unreliable to host prolonged project specific or personal data. Second, there is a need for policy management and capacity management to deal with the growing security concerns and unprecedented data growth. Third, the ability to access data, driven by policy based management, remotely is not present.

To address this, we designed a storage cloud with these characteristics: a *storage service* delivered over a network (Internet or Intranet); economically scaling capacity and performance; easy to manage (e.g. terabytes+); private and driven by enforced policies. At its core, our storage cloud is a middleware layer with virtualized mass storage, allowing the underlying physical storage to be NFS or NAS, shared nothing cluster file systems, or some combination of these. Files created or hosted in our cloud are uniquely identified with a URL so that it can be directly addressed or collectively accessed through a FUSE based virtual directory.

Our storage cloud is implemented with three nodes making use of Xen VMs [6], HDFS [9], NFS and powered by OpenQRM management solution. This remote storage is mounted as a local virtual directory through File System in USErspace (FUSE) [41] modules in Linux and Windows. Apart from the GSD project artifacts, it can also serve other needs like **content collaboration spaces** hosting code repositories, digital content, file archives, streaming media as outlined in the Section 3.

5.3   Lab Any Where(LAW): Online Virtual Labs

Many GSD partners like IT and ITeS organizations face major challenges in aligning their training delivery mechanisms to business objectives. These challenges - related to cost, time, reach, and effectiveness- are prompting organizations to revisit their traditional training delivery modes. Dedicated physical classes don't reach a large audience in offshore and certainly difficult for on-site teams due to logistics related issues. Online e-learning systems provides scalability and rapid delivery but still offshore/on-site people miss "hands-on" experience with real software systems. Other methodologies including Web conference products, terminal emulators, web-based work spaces, Learning Management systems also do not provide "real" interaction with software systems.

Our Lab-Any-Where (LAW) prototype, tries to address this training problem, by making use of cloud principles and components. LAW is a cloud-based application designed to provide *fully-immersive* technical training and software testing labs over network (Intranet or Internet). This Web application also provides richly featured platforms for centrally managing hands-on training and testing scenarios via scheduled and on-demand delivery mechanisms. We make use of virtual appliances in achieving rapid deployment through Web browser interface [38].

Our design prototype is implemented in two modes: one with Microsoft Virtual Server (MVS) for delivering and testing windows OS-based training environments, and the other one with User Mode Linux (UML) for Linux OS-based scenarios. As such, the LAW prototype has two major components: (i) LAW Management that can manage, control and ultimately *orchestrate* lab resources through configurable workflows, scheduling, customization and reporting (2) Delivery component that does automatic deployment through virtual appliances with secure access.

6 Conclusions and Future Work

Clouds represent an inflection point in global distributed software development. The concept draws on many existing technologies and architectures, as we have seen in this paper. Although there is some FUD (Fear, Uncertainty, and Doubt) with all the hype about clouds, we see clouds as a viable and effective platform for offshore and outsourced development in the longer run. In this paper, we outlined some positive indications and resultant implications if they are deployed in a globally distributed software model. However, there are still concerns with respect to vendor lock-in, SLA control, privacy, reliability, data migration & access, auditing and regulation compliance norms. We hope that as the IT industry works to solve these problems, cloud adoption will occur in phases, from the nascent clouds in place today to mature cloud-based platforms with enhanced security and better SLA norms. Moreover, it is our belief that cloud paradigm can provide significant benefits to all key stakeholders in the GSD ecosystem, as evident from the prototypes we showcased here. We also continue to monitor and experiment with the different architectural, programming, and operational models of clouds and share our results with the GSD community. One active area is to explore the ability of clouds to play a game-changing role in software testing. We intend to investigate further into *cloudifying* the testing services as it provides ample scope and ground to check the full potential of cloud paradigm.

References

1. Amazon: Amazon web services for simple db, s3, ec2, http://aws.amazon.com
2. Armbrust, M., Fox, A., Griffith, R., Joseph, A.D., Katz, R., Konwinski, A., Lee, G., Patterson, D., Rabkin, A., Stoica, I., et al.: Above the Clouds: A Berkeley View of Cloud Computing. University of California, Berkeley, Tech. Rep. (2009)
3. Aspray, W., Mayadas, F., Vardi, M.Y.: Globalization and offshoring of software. A Report of the ACM Job Migration Task Force, Executive Summary and Findings. ACM, New York (2006)
4. Atkinson, R.D.: Understanding the offshoring challenge. Progressive Policy Institute, Washington, DC (2004)
5. Baker, S.: Google and the wisdom of clouds. Business Week (2007)
6. Barham, P., Dragovic, B., Fraser, K., Hand, S., Harris, T., Ho, A., Neugebauer, R., Pratt, I., Warfield, A.: Xen and the art of virtualization. ACM SIGOPS Operating Systems Review 37, 164–177 (2003)
7. Battin, R.D., Crocker, R., Kreidler, J., Subramanian, K.: Leveraging resources in global software development. IEEE Softw. 18(2), 70–77 (2001)
8. Bechtolsheim, A.: Cloud Computing and Cloud Networking. talk at UC Berkeley (2008)

9. Bialecki, A., Cafarella, M., Cutting, D., Malley, O.: Hadoop: a framework for running applications on large clusters built of commodity hardware, http://lucene.apache.org/hadoop
10. Buschmann, F.: Pattern-oriented software architecture: a system of patterns. Wiley, Chichester (2002)
11. Buyya, R., Yeo, C.S., Venugopal, S., Ltd, M.P., Melbourne, A.: Market-oriented cloud computing: Vision, hype, and reality for delivering it services as computing utilities. In: Proceedings of the 10th IEEE International Conference on High Performance Computing and Communications (HPCC 2008). IEEE CS Press, Los Alamitos (2008)
12. Chang, F., Dean, J., Ghemawat, S., Hsieh, W.C., Wallach, D.A., Burrows, M., Chandra, T., Fikes, A., Gruber, R.E.: Bigtable: A distributed storage system for structured data. In: Proceedings of the 7th USENIX Symposium on Operating Systems Design and Implementation (OSDI 2006) (2006)
13. Cheng, L.T., de Souza, C.R., Hupfer, S., Patterson, J., Ross, S.: Building collaboration into ides. Queue 1(9), 40–50 (2004)
14. Church, K., Hamilton, J., Greenberg, A.: On delivering embarassingly distributed cloud services. Hotnets VII (2008)
15. Dean, J., Ghemawat, S.: Mapreduce: simplified data processing on large clusters. In: OSDI 2004: Proceedings of the 6th conference on Symposium on Opearting Systems Design & Implementation, Berkeley, CA, USA, p. 10. USENIX Association (2004)
16. Desouza, K., Awazu, Y., Baloh, P.: Managing knowledge in global software development efforts: Issues and practices. IEEE software 23(5), 30–37 (2006)
17. Foster, I., Kesselman, C.: The grid: blueprint for a new computing infrastructure. Morgan Kaufmann, San Francisco (2004)
18. Fryer, K., Gothe, M.: Global software development and delivery: Trends and challenges. IBM Developer Works 1 (January 2008)
19. Ghemawat, S., Gobioff, H., Leung, S.T.: The google file system. In: SOSP 2003: Proceedings of the nineteenth ACM symposium on Operating systems principles, pp. 29–43. ACM, New York (2003)
20. Gillett, E.F., Brown, G.E., Staten, J., Lee, C.: The new tech ecosystems of cloud, cloud services, and cloud computing. Forrester Research Report (August 2008)
21. Google: Google docs and spreadsheets, http://docs.google.com
22. Google: Google's cloud implementation as app engine, http://code.google.com/appengine/
23. Griesemer, R.: Parallelism by design: data analysis with sawzall. In: CGO 2008: Proceedings of the sixth annual IEEE/ACM international symposium on Code generation and optimization, p. 3. ACM, New York (2008)
24. Hamilton, J.: Perspectives blog, http://perspectives.mvdirona.com
25. Herbsleb, J.D., Mockus, A.: An empirical study of speed and communication in globally distributed software development. IEEE Transactions on Software Engineering 29(6), 481–494 (2003)
26. Herbsleb, J., Moitra, D.: Global software development. IEEE software 18(2), 16–20 (2001)
27. Huhns, M.N., Singh, M.P.: Service-oriented computing: Key concepts and principles. IEEE Internet Computing 9(1), 75–81 (2005)
28. Krishna, S., Sahay, S., Walsham, G.: Managing cross-cultural issues in global software outsourcing. Communications of the ACM 47(4), 62–66 (2004)
29. Lin, G., Fu, D., Zhu, J., Dasmalchi, G.: Cloud computing: It as a service. IT Professional 11(2), 10–13 (2009)

30. Meijer, E., Beckman, B., Bierman, G.: LINQ: reconciling object, relations and XML in the.NET framework. In: Proceedings of the 2006 ACM SIGMOD international conference on Management of data, p. 706. ACM, New York (2006)
31. Meyer, B., Hochschule, E.T., Zurich, S.: The unspoken revolution in software engineering. IEEE Computer 39(1), 124 (2006)
32. Microsoft-Live: Microsoft live mesh api, http://www.mesh.com
33. Montoya-Weiss, M., Massey, A., Song, M.: Getting it together: Temporal coordination and conflict management in global virtual teams. Academy of Management Journal, 1251–1262 (2001)
34. Olson, J.S., Olson, G.M.: Culture surprises in remote software development teams. Queue 1(9), 52–59 (2004)
35. Olston, C., Reed, B., Srivastava, U., Kumar, R., Tomkins, A.: Pig Latin: A not-so-foreign language for data processing. In: Proceedings of the 2008 ACM SIGMOD international conference on Management of data, pp. 1099–1110. ACM, New York (2008)
36. Rangan, K.: The Cloud Wars: $100+ billion at stake. Technical report, Tech. rep., Merrill Lynch (2008)
37. ReductiveLabs: Puppet configuration management, http://reductivelabs.com/trac/puppet
38. Rosenblum, M., Garfinkel, T.: Virtual machine monitors: Current technology and future trends. IEEE Computer 38(5), 39–47 (2005)
39. Salesforce: Salesforce customer relationships management (crm) system, http://www.salesforce.com/
40. Siegele, L.: Let It Rise: A Special Report on Corporate IT. The Economist (October 2008)
41. Szeredi, M.: Filesystem in userspace, http://fuse.sourceforge.net
42. Thain, D., Tannenbaum, T., Livny, M.: Distributed computing in practice: The Condor experience. Concurrency and Computation: Practice and Experience 17(2-4), 323–356 (2005)
43. Uhlig, R., Neiger, G., Rodgers, D., Santoni, A.L., Martins, F.C.M., Anderson, A.V., Bennett, S.M., Kagi, A., Leung, F.H., Smith, L.: Intel virtualization technology. IEEE Computer 38, 48–56 (2005)
44. Vogels, W.: A Head in the Clouds - The Power of Infrastructure as a Service. In: First workshop on Cloud Computing and in Applications (CCA 2008) (October 2008)
45. Weiss, A.: Computing in the clouds. ACM net Worker 11(4), 16–25 (2007)

Competitive Risk Identification Method for Distributed Teams

Yegor Bugayenko

TechnoPark Corp.
568 9th Street South 202
Naples, Florida 34102
egor@technoparkcorp.com

Abstract. The described method is a risk identification scenario for software development projects, where the project team is multi-lingual and distributed, time for the risk identification meeting is limited, meetings are recurrent and an amount of risks required is bigger than a hundred. The meeting is conducted as an online chat game, where participants compete for each risk source, inventing the most severe risk. The winner gets a bonus, while the meeting facilitator gets a big list of raw risks.

Keywords: Risk Management, Distributed Team, Risk Identification, Distributed Meetings.

1 Introduction

One of the most important "process area" in project management is risk management, which includes risk planning, risk identification, qualitative and quantitative analysis, risk response planning and risk monitoring [1]. The risk identification process provides the material for risk analysis and risk response planning. A raw list of risks, that shall include hundreds of them [2, pp. 61–102], can be generated by different methods, including brainstorming [3], historical records, checklists and templates [4], risk charting, objectives-based, scenario-based, taxonomy-based [5], conduct a "pre-mortem" [6], Affinity Diagrams [7, pp. 135–141], Delphi technique [8,9], expert interviews, Nominal Group Technique [10,11], and others.

Every method has its own advantages and drawbacks [12,16,13,14,15]. However, any of them when applied to a project with the following constraints, will fail to produce a required result: a) project team is multi-lingual and distributed (online text chats only), b) risk identification meetings must take less than one hour, c) meetings are held regularly (every iteration), and d) each meeting shall produce at least a hundrend risks.

Existing methods will fail in these circumstances because of (most common causes): a) Inattention; b) Language barriers; c) Unavoidable personal criticism; d) Weariness after repeating meetings; and e) Untrained risk identifiers.

A good solution to the outlined problems could be a method that will reduce the amount of efforts required for risk identification, at the same time increasing personnel engagement and motivation.

O. Gotel, M. Joseph, and B. Meyer (Eds.): SEAFOOD 2009, LNBIP 35, pp. 96–101, 2009.

2 Method

The purpose of this method is to increase the effectiveness of risk identification meetings in software development projects, reduce the time and effort required for the meetings and make the meetings possible to be held in online text chat form.

The meeting facilitator prepares and presents to the meeting participants the list of five key project objectives and a list of risk sources (up to dozen). The objectives go horizontally, while risk sources vertically. The matrix becomes a field for the Risk Game.

The rules of the Risk Game are:

1. Facilitator announces the next row (risk source);
2. Everyone invents risks for the given risk source;
3. Facilitator chooses the winner for the row;
4. Matrix gets the name of the winner in a corresponding cell;
5. The person who has the most cells wins the game.

The meeting recorder maintans the list of all invented risks. This list is passed to the facilitator by the end of the meeting. The result of the Risk Game is a long list of raw unsorted risks, which will be used by the project management for quantitative and qualitative risk analysis.

The proposed method is more effective than other existing methods when meeting time is limited (less than one hour) and a big list of risks is required (more than a hundred). The method is more effective in such circumstances because it quickly involves everybody in the process, converts individual cricism into a fair competition and stimulates group thinking.

3 Practical Example

Figure 1 illustrates a workflow of the method, starting with the definition of project objectives, risk sources and a list of meeting participants (101). Project objectives are the most important "targets" that the project has to achieve in order to be successfully closed. Risk sources are facts that may become root causes of risks. Sources are something that already happened, while risks are events that may happen and have negative (or positive) effects for at least one project objectives.

It's desired to have a limited number of project objectives (up to 5) and a limited amount of risk sources (less than a dozen). Bigger numbers will make the risk identification meeting too long and not so effective, mostly because participants won't stay focused.

The facilitator asks all meeting participants to draw a risk matrix (example is on Figure 2), where horizontally they place project objectives and vertically risk sources. Each meeting participant has such a matrix locally (we assume that the meeting is help in a virtual online chat environment).

Then the meeting goes in iterative manner, from risk source to risk source, down the risk matrix. For each next row in a matrix the facilitator announces a

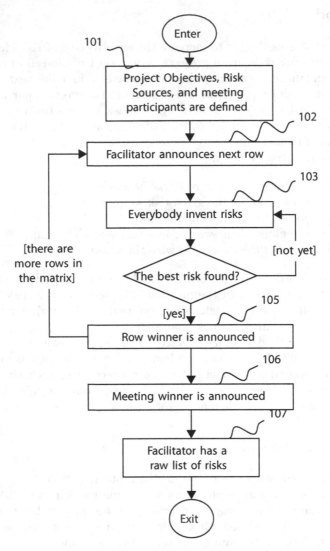

Fig. 1. Method flow chart that illustrates interconnections between key activities of the described method. The activities are performed during one risk identification meetings taking totally 40-60 minutes.

risk source (102) and asks meeting participants to invent and propose possible risks. The risks identified should have the declared source and should affect one or more project objectives. Meeting participants invent risks (103) and send them in more or less universal format to the chat.

The faciliator waits until the best risk is found, according to his/her own understanding and criteria. As soon as such a risk is found, facilitator announces the winner of the row (105) and goes to the next row.

	Project achieves all baselined objectives in budget	Proof-of-concept prototype is deployed to users on 10-Aug	Web site performance of 500 pages per second	Test code coverage measured by LoC is over 80%	Over 150 critical defects discovered and fixed
Lack of technical experience in used technologies (J2EE and Web Services)	4	2	3	4	1
Budget shortage (underestimated project)	2	3	1	2	3
Vague end-user requirements	3	4	1	1	2
Distributed and multi-lingual team	1	3	4	2	6
Deployment platform is provided by customer and is not ready yet	2	3	7	2	4
Half of project team members are new workers to Project Manager	3	4	0	0	1

Fig. 2. Risk Game Matrix is a key artifact used during the Risk Game. Risk Sources are listed vertically and Project Objectives are listed horizontally. Cells of the matrix include numbers of risks suggested by meeting participants and recorded by the meeting facilitator.

At the end of the meeting the facilitator announces the winner of the meeting (106) – the person who won the most of rows. The most important result of the meeting is the raw list of risks (107), which will be long enough for any project size.

A full-scale identification meeting with a team of 6-10 participants shall take 40-60 minutes, if the facilitator has some experience of using the method. The meeting goes in a very aggressive and competitive manner, challenging all participants and getting the maximum of their creativity. Even better meeting performance could be achieved by means of a monetized award to the meeting winner.

Figure 2 is a sample risk matrix, used during a risk identification meeting. Horizontally it has a list of project objectives and vertically a list of risk sources. Cells of the matrix are placeholders for risk, identified during the meeting.

In total, there were 70 risks identified with this matrix. It is important to note that the amount of risks identified does not say anything about how "risky" the project is. The only thing it indicates is the quality of risk identification outcome.

It is known that any software product has an unlimited amount of defects [17, pp. 9–20]. A similar statement is applicable to risk identification: "Any project has an unlimited amount of risks". The task for the project manager is to identify the most critical of them.

Using the proposed method risk identification may be a very iterative and repetitive process. If project manager feels that there is not enough risks identified in the risk list, he/she can organize additional risk identification meetings, make some changes to the Risk Game Matrix and make some changes to the meeting team. A new meeting will produce new useful raw list of risks.

4   Conclusion and Future Research

The described method was invented and implemented in TechnoPark Corp. in June 2008. Since that time the method was applied to seven commercial projects. In total, 40+ risk identification meetings using this method have been already conducted. In comparison with previous projects a number of advantages were received:

- We enabled an effective distributed and multi-lingual risk discussions and identification;
- Risk management is not a boring bureaucracy any longer, but is a challenging game. All team members stay focused on risks and their pro-active identification;
- We significantly reduce project expenses due to much more throrough risk identification;
- We keep risk identification meeting protocols in text files accessible for all project participants, including the customer. Thus, we optimize communication and avoid loss of information.

In the next years we are going to collect more numeric results afer the method application and give more formal proof of its effectiveness. We are also thinking about inventing a similar method for risk response planning.

References

1. Project Management Institute, Project Management Body of Knowledge (PM-BOK) Guide v.3., 3rd edn. PMI Press (2004)
2. Mulcahy, R.: Risk Management, Tricks of the Trade for Project Managers. RMC Publications, Inc., USA (2003)
3. Osborn, A.F.: Applied imagination: Principles and procedures of creative problem solving, 3rd revised edn. Charles Scribner's Sons, New York (1963)
4. National Cyber Security Division of the U.S. Department of Homeland Security, Common vulnerabilities and exposures, Technical report, The MITRE Corporation, USA (2008)
5. Carr, M.J., Kondra, S.L., Monarch, I., Ulrich, F.C., Walker, C.F.: Taxonomy-based risk identification, Technical Report CMU/SEI-93-TR-006, Software Engineering Institute, Carnegie Mellon University, Pittsburgh, Pennsylvania, USA (1993)
6. Mitchell, J.E.R., Deborah, J., Pennington, N.: Back to the future: Temporal perspective in the explanation of events. Journal of Behavioral Decision Making 2, 25–39 (1989)

7. Britz, G.C., Emerling, D.W., Hare, L.B., Hoerl, R.W., Janis, S.J., Shade, J.E.: Improving Performance Through Statistical Thinking. American Society for Quality, USA (2000)

8. Linstone, H.A., Turoff, M.: The Delphi Method: Techniques and Applications. New Jersey's Science & Technology University, NJ, USA (1975)

9. Schmidt, R., Lyytinen, K., Keil, M., Cule, P.: Identifying software project risks: An international delphi study. Journal of Management of Information Systems 17(4), 5–36 (2001)

10. Delbecq, A.L., VandeVen, A.H.: A group process model for problem identification and program planning. Journal Of Applied Behavioral Science VII, 466–491 (July/August 1971)

11. Delbecq, A.L., VandeVen, A.H., Gustafson, D.H.: Group Techniques for Program Planners. Scott Foresman and Company, Glenview, Illinois (1975)

12. Freimut, B., Hartkopf, S., Kaiser, P., Kontio, J., Kobitzsch, W.: An industrial case study of implementing software risk management. In: ESEC/FSE-9: Proceedings of the 8th European software engineering conference held jointly with 9th ACM SIGSOFT international symposium on Foundations of software engineering, New York, NY, USA, pp. 277–287 (2001)

13. Keil, M., Cule, P.E., Lyytinen, K., Schmidt, R.C.: A framework for identifying software project risks. Communications of the ACM 41(11), 76–83 (1998)

14. Wallace, L., Keil, M.: Software project risks and their effect on outcomes. Communications of the ACM 47(4), 68–73 (2004)

15. Fairley, R.E.: Software risk management. IEEE Software 22(3), 101 (2005)

16. Charette, R.N.: Software engineering risk analysis and management. McGraw-Hill, Inc., New York (1989)

17. Myers, G.J.: The Art of Software Testing, 2nd edn. John Wiley & Sons, Inc., NJ (2004)

Model-Centric Approach to Software Design and Stakeholder-Specific Architecture Views in Scope of a Financial Institution

Patrick Senti

Senior Software Engineer
CREDIT SUISSE AG,
IT Private Banking, P.O. Box, 8070 Zurich, Switzerland
patrick.senti@credit-suisse.com

Abstract. This paper presents a model-centric approach to software architecture & design in the scope of a large financial institution. One challenge in large organizations is the creation, aggregation and dissemination of architecture and design specifications by multiple stakeholders and outsourcing partners, at different times during the lifecycle of a software application. Lacking a common design language and format, the submission of manually written reports is common, which in turn facilitates redundancies in content and causes specifications at large to become cluttered, inconsistent and difficult to maintain. Manually written reports also tend to focus designers on producing nicely arranged diagrams and prosaic description, rather than on applying sound principles of software engineering. In turn, such specifications frustrate their subsequent use for coding, effectively rendering the design effort questionable. The approach presented defines a model-centric approach to enable different architecture views, based on models maintained by a team of designers. Employing a single-source concept, the same models serve the purpose of software design, coding and stakeholder-specific reports.

Keywords: UML in Software Engineering, Stakeholder Views, Architecture Documentation.

1 Introduction

This paper first describes the business-implied importance of information technology for financial institutions. It briefly looks at the reasons and implications, and in particular elaborates how various concerns exist in relation to IT systems used by financial institutions in general, and in particular as is the case at Credit Suisse AG, Switzerland, within its IT Private Banking division. In mapping the concerns to IEEE Standard 1471 and other contributions to software architecture documentation, I present an analysis of the information needs that are derived from these concerns. Next, I offer the observation that the usual setup found in larger organizations – that is, to request and provide document-based, manually written reports to address these concerns – is negatively impacting both the quality of documentation of IT systems,

O. Gotel, M. Joseph, and B. Meyer (Eds.): SEAFOOD 2009, LNBIP 35, pp. 102–116, 2009.

and the productivity of software engineers. In the subsequent sections, I first outline an alternative approach to creating IT system documentation, whereby the information needs by stakeholders of IT systems are abstracted into a common metamodel and stakeholder-specific reports are defined in terms of this metamodel. In the next chapter, I then analyze the requirements and derive the design for a system to implement this approach. The result is a model-centric system, "TSDOC". TSDOC leverages OMG's Unified Modeling Language (UML) and provides the means for successful collaboration among software engineers and outsourcing partners. I proclaim that TSDOC enables software engineers to eliminate redundancy in system documentation. In the last section, I describe the ongoing implementation of TSDOC at Credit Suisse and summarize the lessons learnt so far.

1.1 Importance of IT Systems for Financial Institutions

For financial institutions, information technology has long become a key element of operating the business. Almost all transactions executed by financial institutions generate or modify data. Data in this sense includes customer data, account data, stock and other financial market data, credit data or economic data. The data needs to be processed according to laws and regulations, and the steps taken in processing the data must be accounted for at all times – which generates even further data (e.g. audit trails). In short, financial institutions of practically any size and scope have no alternative but to rely on IT systems.

Therefore, financial institutions must not only manage the economic risks inherent in the business itself, but they must also ensure that their IT systems[1] operate reliably, predictably and uninterrupted. At the same time, it is a non-disputable requirement that the systems operate consistent with all the laws and regulations - whichever jurisdiction applies to any one particular transaction - as well as company-internal policies. Further, all activities must be accounted for in terms of transaction logs. Last but not least, IT systems must be developed and operated cost-effectively, especially in light of new business needs, a changing regulatory environment and frequent updates and advances of information technology in general.

1.2 Organizational Roles as Stakeholders of Systems

As a means of proper governance of these varied aspects, organizations have identified and assigned responsibilities to respective organizational roles. At Credit Suisse, these roles include: IT Enterprise Architects, IT Security Architects, Solution Architects, Solution Engineers (co-located and offshore), IT Risk Officers, Business Continuity Management and IT Operations staff. In the context of both, a) the compound of all IT systems ("system of systems"), and b) the context of one particular IT system, these organizational roles belong to the group of stakeholders of the IT systems used in the organization. Specifically, the roles are stakeholders *of any an IT system's architecture*. Hence, architects must take into account these stakeholders and address their concerns when designing and developing IT systems.

---

[1] For the purpose of this paper, the term "IT system" refers to what is the scope of IEEE Std 1471 [1]: *"software-intensive systems – any system in which software development and/or integration are dominant considerations (...)"*

1.3 Documentation Standards Address Stakeholder Concerns

The need to address concerns of multiple stakeholders has been described in the literature and is the subject of standardization efforts. For example, the IEEE Standard 1471 [1] recommends to look at an IT system's architecture from many different perspectives, each of which serves the particular concerns of one or multiple stakeholders. The metamodel presented in IEEE Standard 1471 is depicted in figure 1. Many models and methods [2][3] have been proposed and indeed influenced the creation of this standard [4].

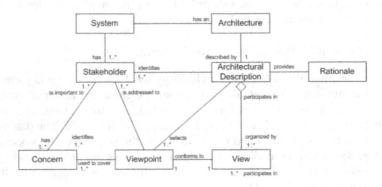

Fig. 1. IEEE 1471-2000 Metamodel

Models such as the IEEE Standard 1471 [1], Kruchten's 4+1 view model [2], TOGAF [4] or Zachman [5] each provide a particular set of definitions of what the specific architecture documentation should contain, on varying levels of details. They share, however, one commonality: all describe the architecture documentation as a compound of multiple views to a system's design. Views in this context typically depict and describe a particular aspect which is based on the system's structural elements (static view), its processes and data flows (dynamic view) or the system's hardware and software operating environment (deployment view).

1.4 Context of System Specification and Documentation at Credit Suisse

Credit Suisse has defined a standardized set of deliverables that software development projects are required to produce. The standard is enforced through a formal project lifecycle with five distinct milestones[2]. At each milestone, projects are required to deliver a specific set of results ("work products"), based on formal templates defined in the context of the applicable processes (SEI-certified at CMMI Level 2). All major work products such as the project plan, the requirements specification, the system's design and architecture, the IT operations concept (as a compound referred to as "the system architecture documentation") are reviewed by the IT system's stakeholders, who are organized in the Project Review Board (PRB). The PRB members perform a

---

[2] For projects executed in Switzerland, the milestones are: PC [Project Concept], PO [Project Offer], RO [Realization Offer], RD [Ready for Deployment], RC [Request for Conclusion]. Other sites apply different milestones, but follow a similar concept.

formal review and either approve, approve with obligations or reject a project's deliverables.

1.4.1 Large-Scale Application Landscape and Institutionalized Governance

Credit Suisse, in Switzerland, operates more than 750 applications, totaling over 40 million lines of code. The applications are based on an IBM mainframe infrastructure (majority of transactions processing and data persistency), and the internally developed, J2EE-/Unix-based application platform (internet, intranet, workflow). Applications are connected by an enterprise service bus based on a set of synchronous and asynchronous messaging middleware.

Many of these applications have been developed and continuously adopted to new business requirements over the last 20 years, in some cases for more than 30 years. Changes to applications are based on requests by the bank's business lines. Requests are assigned to projects, which then take responsibility for development, testing and deployment of new application releases. In any particular year, a portfolio of several hundred projects are executed.

Formal architecture governance ensures the continuous, managed evolution of the systems in-line with business needs and based on technology standards applied throughout Credit Suisse [11]. The architecture organization has been institutionalized at the level of the enterprise, at regional level and within the lines of business ("application domains").

1.4.2 Globally Distributed Workforce, Outsourced Offshore Development

Credit Suisse IT operates regional centers in USA (Raleigh & New York), Europe (Zurich & London) and Asia (Singapore). Overall, up to 40% of work is contractually outsourced, and the collaboration with preferred offshore partners (located in India) is common practice.

Credit Suisse is applying its processes throughout the full application portfolio: That is, the same processes apply to in-house environments as well as to work which is outsourced to offshore partners. In order to ensure the quality of work, the handover of responsibility for deliverables between Credit Suisse and the partner organization follows a pre-defined procedure. For example, the procedure defines one handover to take place at milestone RO ("realization offer"), where the responsibility to detail a system's specification is transferred from Credit Suisse to the outsourcing partner. Upon deployment of the system (milestone RD), the responsibility is transferred back to Credit Suisse. The same is true for other deliverables such as the source code, build files, test scripts or further documentation. The overall responsibility for the project in terms of project management and quality assessment remains with Credit Suisse at all times.

1.4.3 Analysis of Stakeholder Needs at Credit Suisse

In order to understand and formally classify the information needs of the Credit Suisse stakeholders, an in-depth analysis has been performed by means of interviewing stakeholder representatives, and analyzing existing specification documents. The interview participants were nominated by the line and functional management to represent their organizational unit and/or a particular community of stakeholders. For each stakeholder group, two representatives were interviewed. The interviews were conducted in order to understand the current challenges faced by the stakeholders, in relation to system documentation and respective collaboration with projects. A second goal was to identify potential redundancies in the set of documentation that is normally requested of projects.

1.4.4 Common Needs, Duplication of Content

The interviews and the study of existing documentation showed that different stakeholders request similar data, but in different contexts and sometimes from differing points of view, as is summarized in Fig. 2.

For example, most stakeholders request a system context diagram and a component overview to be included, and all stakeholders request to understand the deployment of the application onto the IT systems infrastructure. However, this common need had not been previously identified, which has caused the same information elements to be seen as different from each other. This situation has resulted in duplication of information by "copy/paste" and, over time, has lead to inconsistencies in the documentation of many systems. This is particularly true in the case of re-assigned responsibility when, over time, systems have been modified by different teams. It is equally true when responsibility is shared by teams, co-located or offshore, possibly working on multiple releases of the system (e.g. maintenance and new release).

	System Specification	System Spec Security	IT Operations	IT Operations Manual	IT DR Concept	IT Risk Profile	PO/RO (Sol Concept)
System Overview	x	x	x			x	x
Components	x	x	x		x		x
Nodes	x	x	x	x			
Network	x					x	
Interfaces	x	x	x			x	
Batch Model	x		x	x		x	
Data/Information Model	x					x	
Role/Security		x	(x)	x		x	
Restart procedures			(x)	x	x		
Monitoring procedures			x	x		x	
Testing						x	
Risk assessments	x	x				x	x
Storage requirements				x			
Output and Archiving			x	x			
Platform/Deployment	x	x	x	x	x	x	x

Fig. 2. Currently requested reports by stakeholders, mapped to results of system design

With this approach, keeping documents in synchronization has become a hopeless endeavor. In turn, software engineers are required to research and collect documentation from various sources, and often find there is no up-to-date view of a system's design that corresponds to the actual implementation. This lack of readily available documentation is costly. It also causes productivity to suffer because software engineers need to spend an inappropriate amount of time to analyze systems prior to implementing changes.

1.5 Challenges to Address

In summary, several challenges were identified based on the interviews conducted with representatives of the stakeholder groups at Credit Suisse:

- "Documentation of applications inconsistent or not up-to-date": Over time, applications have been changed by different projects and different people, who used different documentation standards and formats. This is perceived as a risk of losing important knowledge when key employees leave the company or are assigned to different tasks.
- "Loss of productivity": The non-availability of a current set of documentation results in projects having to invest time to search, consolidate, re-engineer and validate an application's documentation prior to planning and effecting changes.
- "Technical specifications insufficient for implementation": As technical specifications are often captured in the form of non-formalized textual documents, outsourcing and offshore partners sometimes are required to substantially refine the specifications in order to meet expectations. This carries the risk of avoidable cost of communication and delays.

Note that all challenges were identified in terms of qualitative criteria only, based on the needs identified and prioritized by the stakeholder groups as described in section 1.4.3.

2 A Model-Centric Approach: TSDOC

To address these challenges, a new approach should enable to reduce redundancies, and improve the quality of specifications. As systems change, documentation should be updated continuously, by collaboration across teams, locations, projects and time.

The approach outlined in this chapter uses UML as a means to improve specifications. Configuration management is applied to enable collaboration in teams and with offshore partners, as well as to manage the UML models across system releases, comparable to source code. To reduce information redundancy, stakeholder-specific information needs are abstracted into views, such that the views can re-use the same UML models.

As a concept, the use of UML models as input to architecture views is described by Kruchten [6], where the Software Architecture Document (SAD) is defined as the architecturally significant subset of a system's models used for specification.

Fig. 3. Architecture View as a subset of analysis and design models

In order to address the various stakeholder information concerns, however, there is no single architecture view: rather, each stakeholder's viewpoint in turn is a specific subset of the overall architecture view as depicted in Fig 4.

2.1 Related Work

In identifying the contents of each stakeholder-specific subset of the architecture view, using an established approach is helpful. Related work includes Hilliard [9],

Egyed/Medvidovic [8] and Hofmeister et al. [10], who describe the use of UML elements for architectural views, while Clements et al. [7] provide an approach to software architecture documentation in accordance with IEEE Standard 1471-2000. In terms of the overall concept of choosing, developing and representing architectural views, Credit Suisse have used the approach as described by Clements et al. This was combined with the analysis and design discipline described by Kruchten [6], in particular the use of models to specify systems.

Since the use of UML, as such, to represent multiple *architectural* views (i.e. static, dynamic and deployment views) is well established, I shall focus on the needs implied by using UML models to support multiple *stakeholder* views.

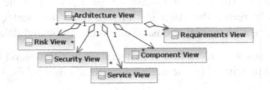

Fig. 4. Multiple views of a system's architecture, representing stakeholder information needs

2.2   Architecture Documentation – A System in Itself

I propose to take a systemic approach to software documentation. The approach implies that UML models form the central element of all documentation, such that the concerns of designers are separated from the concerns of the stakeholders, who ask for a particular subset or aggregated information based on the design. In particular, I propose to look at the requirements in regards to the architecture documentation as a system in itself. This system henceforward is referred to as "TSDOC".

2.2.1   Use Cases of TSDOC
In terms of TSDOC, I consider the following major use cases [Actor -> Use Case]: 1. [Software Architect -> Create the analysis and design models]; 2. [Software Engineer -> Contribute to existing models (configuration management, model merges)]; 3. [Software Architect -> Define and publish concrete architecture views, based on the models]; 4. [Application Owner -> Manage models and views in scope of the system's lifecycle]; 5. [Process Engineer/Stakeholders -> Define template views and respective views, in terms of the metamodel].

In analyzing these use cases, the responsibilities to be handled by components of TSDOC are:

1. To enable to create and manage UML models, using UML
2. To enable collaboration and configuration management;
3. To enable the (concrete) definition and publication of stakeholder views;
4. To enable the (abstract) definition of template views in terms of the metamodel;
5. To manage the metamodel itself.

2.2.2 Design of TSDOC

In TSDOC, the following coarse-grained components provide these facilities (Fig. 5.):

1. ModelingTool;
2. CollaborationEngine;
3. DocumentPublisher;
4. ReleaseManager;
5. UMLProfileManager.

The ModelingTool component is used to create analysis, design and deployment models, using UML, based on the common metamodel derived from stakeholder needs. The metamodel is provided in the form of a UML profile. The CollaborationEngine allows for multiple designers to work on models in parallel. The DocumentPublisher (1) allows the definition of stakeholder-specific views in terms and by relation of elements found in the UML models, and (2) provides a generator/model-transformation that processes the view definition to (3) create formatted, printable reports. The ReleaseManager collects all relevant models, view definitions and reports into a documentation release format, very much like source code is compiled into a deployable software package. The UMLProfileManager, in fact a sub-component of the ModelingTool, defines a UML Profile as the metamodel and ensures its usability by the other components.

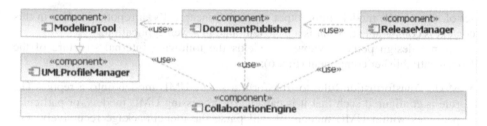

Fig. 5. The TSDOC component model (Overview)

2.2.3 Separating Stakeholder-Specific Views from Design Models

The collection of all UML models created by component designers is used as the basis for the stakeholder-specific reports. However, in most stakeholder reports, many of the details required to implement the software are not of interest. Rather, stakeholder reports tend to require a somewhat aggregated, summarized level of information. For example, the internal classes of component A are not usually a concern of the Enterprise Architect, whereas the dependencies of component A to other components and systems within the larger enterprise are of interest.

As each of the stakeholder views addresses different sets of concerns, the DocumentPublisher component of TSDOC is considered separate from the ModelingTool. The DocumentPublisher should be configurable such that multiple stakeholder reports can be generated from the same set of source UML models. In order to do so, the DocumentPublisher requires the definition of views in terms of a generic report template. The template follows a set of pre-defined rules to transform a

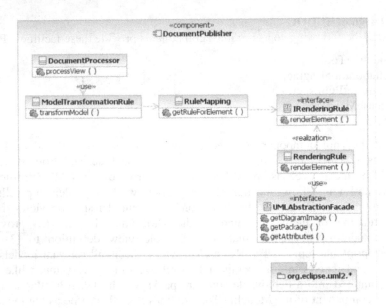

Fig. 6. Internal design of DocumentPublisher component

set of input UML models into output reports. Conceptually, a report template in this context is comparable to what is a page template in a web application.

From a design point of view, this yields the following internal structure of the DocumentPublisher component (Fig. 6):

- ModelTransformationRule, to transform a set of UML models into a report. The rule is configured such that it is capable of processing UML models, or particular packages within UML models. It will parse the model/package recursively. For each element found, it will invoke an instance of a RenderingRule. The way the ModelTransformationRule knows about Rendering-Rules is by looking at the RuleMappings, which map model elements to RenderingRules.
- RenderingRule. A RenderingRule is a script that will take a model element as input, and render formatted, printable output. Usually, this output is in a format such as HTML, XML, DocBook, RTF - in principle, the output can be in any format required. RenderingRules can be thought as working much similar to templates written using Sun's JavaServer Pages (JSP) or Microsoft's Application Server Pages (ASP) technology.
- UMLAbstractionFacade, which abstracts the UML metamodel and APIs provided by Eclipse's GMF. It does so for the RenderingRules to have a simple, straight forward API that does not imply specific knowledge about GMF. For example, the facade will provide methods such as getImage(), getPackage() or getAttributes() to allow for retrieval of model content and visual elements by name.
- RuleMapping, which implements a mapping of model elements to RenderingRules. A mapping can be by name of model element, by naming convention, by model element types or stereotypes.

- DocumentProcessor, whose purpose is to transform combined output of all triggered RenderingRules into a format suitable for deployment or printing (HTML, PDF). It is called upon start of a model transformation, and finally to finish the output processing. RenderingRules should be able to call the DocumentProcessor to notify of certain properties (such as particular style sheets to apply etc.)

2.2.4 Rationale for Systemic Approach vs. Standard UML Tools

One could argue that it is unnecessary to look at architecture documentation as a system by itself, since most available UML modeling tools provide a concrete implementation of such a design already. In a sense, this is true: many UML modeling tools indeed provide the facilities to tackle the above identified use cases.

However, practitioners tend to loose sight of the separation of the concerns apparent from TSDOC's use cases. In turn, the different concerns often are intermixed, and in conclusion there is no longer a clear separation of a metamodel, concrete UML models and views. Further, while most tools provide a component similar to the DocumentPublisher as defined above, this is not usually configured for enterprise use: instead, it is assumed that each designer will define concrete reports based on concrete UML models. This results in tightly coupled report definitions that themselves reflect the structure of the models (e.g. such a report definition would rely on the design model to provide a package "A" or a component "B"; when the design changes, the report definition has to be changed accordingly). Therefore, re-use of generic, stakeholder-specific report/view templates becomes impossible. However, reuse of modeling templates and stakeholder reports is a requirement in any larger organization, for economic reasons as well as for the purpose of effective governance.

Taking a step back in separating the various concerns thus helps to make better use of the UML modeling tools, in particular in an enterprise setting.

2.3 Common Metamodel of Stakeholder Views

In order to formalize the stakeholder views a common metamodel is required. The metamodel serves as the common language to define, on an abstract level, the contents of each view. The information needs identified in the analysis   were subsequently aggregated, essentially forming a metamodel of the various stakeholder reports. Using this metamodel, it is now possible, for example, to formally define the context diagram – requested by multiple stakeholders - as being made of "Applications", and the "InformationFlows" between these "Applications".

The metamodel at Credit Suisse is loosely based on the concepts and terminology found in the analysis and design discipline described by Kruchten, extended to meet specific needs of Credit Suisse. The metamodel was subsequently transformed into a UML Profile to facilitate the modeling of systems using the very terminology.

2.4 Collaborative Design: Model Ownership Is Essential

Based on the collaboration capabilities of the tool environment (e.g. configuration management and distributed versioning systems), all design activities can be distributed among co-located team members and outsourcing partners at offshore locations. Configuration management further ensures that all UML models are managed, over time, as part of the system's releases (similar to its source code).

As with any collaborative effort, it is essential to define ownership of artifacts, in this case in relation to the UML models. The process to do so is essentially identical to that of defining ownership with respect to component-level source code: 1. define the major components, 2. assign ownership of components, 3. define the procedure to commit changes and updates, in particular in the case of conflicts and required merges. Note that for the purpose of efficient collaboration, and to enable non-conflicting ownership assignment, the names, number and structure of UML models should at best correlate with the component design of the IT system in question.

Once ownership has been assigned, the designers focus on the component(s) assigned to them. To do so, they will take the existing UML model(s) of the respective component, or create a new model. Essentially, designers have complete freedom in respect of the internal design of a particular component (reflected in the respective UML model) - within the limits given by the system's requirements and constraints. Once this work is completed, all component models are collected and integrated within the system-level UML models.

2.5 Stakeholder Views Reference Component Models

The models created by component owners are meant to be of use for coding (code generation) and system integration: thus, these models should address the concerns of software developers. Stakeholder views, in contrast, will reference those abstractions and levels of detail that match the concerns of the respective stakeholder. If needed, further abstractions can be added to the system-level UML models to trace elements from stakeholder views to the component-level design models and vice-versa.

2.6 Scalability Requires Automation

In light of the size of Credit Suisse's Private Banking IT unit, there is a need for the standardization of the software development environment. While the development tools as such (IDEs, compilers, debuggers, RDBMS etc.) have traditionally been provided along the computing platforms, the use and standardization of a design environment has only been recently initiated. Along with that comes the need to provide automation for common tasks, including the set-up of models, the collaboration and configuration management facilities, and the automation of view publishing.

To this end, TSDOC as implemented at Credit Suisse provides a set of scripts that automate the creation of model projects, as well as the publishing of stakeholder views. A usage guideline explains the environment to the novice, and step-by-step instructions support the solution architects in using the tools as efficiently as possible.

2.7 UML Models Annotated, External Documents Attached

Using TSDOC, solution architects create well-defined UML models annotated by descriptions and diagrams, instead of writing textual documents intermixed with (often: free-form) graphics. The UML models, in turn, serve as the basis for several reports defined in stakeholder views. The views are UML models themselves, but contain UML diagrams that reference elements from other models, to be included in the stakeholder views. External documents such as text documents or graphics are attachable to UML models or stakeholder views by means of URI-formatted shortcuts. The reports are printed as a direct representation of the view models, that is each package in the model corresponds to a document chapter or sub-chapter.

2.8 Implementation by Commercial Product Suite

The IBM Rational Software Development Platform (SDP) provides a full-fledged, integrated software engineering and development environment. At Credit Suisse, TSDOC is currently implemented based on the SDP, using the Rational Software Modeler as its ModelingTool, Rational Clearcase as its CollaborationEngine, Apache Ant scripts as its ReleaseManager and Rational SoDA as the DocumentPublisher. As the SDP is based on Eclipse, TSDOC uses custom-developed Eclipse plugins to distribute a UML profile, effectively realizing the common metamodel (compare section 1.4.3), a set of standardized model templates, stakeholder view templates, and automation scripts.

3   Experience and Lessons Learnt

The implementation of TSDOC at Credit Suisse has started in January 2009, by means of five projects piloting this approach. The results so far are encouraging in terms of the applicability of the approach for both creating specifications and documenting existing systems, as well as for producing respective stakeholder views. However, it is too early to deduce any significant results in terms of effects on productivity or design quality. Nevertheless, first implications and lessons learnt are described below. These were derived from feedbacks received in writing and insight gained from discussions with participating employees.

3.1   Validation by Piloting Projects

The piloting projects have been selected to be representative of typical projects. As Table 1 indicates most employees participating did not have prior experience using UML or UML-based modeling tools, which is assumed to be the common situation for most projects at large. However, all participating employees are experienced in designing and specifying systems using non-formal, document-based approaches.

3.2   Lessons Learnt

Despite the early stage of implementation, there are a number of concerns and lessons learnt that can be drawn from the piloting projects, as outlined in the following sections.

3.2.1   Use of UML Modeling Perceived as Useful

All participants approve of the use of UML models as the main means of specification and documentation. According to their feedback, one advantage lies in the ability to

Table 1. Projects piloting TSDOC. Platform indicates the technology platform (Java=J2EE, Mainframe=IBM zOS); UML Experience indicates knowledge of UML/UML-tools of the responsible solution architect; Status indicates status of the analysis and design work in the project (discontinued = project was stopped for reasons not connected to TSDOC); #Employees indicates the number of employees directly using TSDOC's modeling approach.

	Project 1	Project 2	Project 3	Project 4	Project 5
Type	New System	Change to system	Change to system	Re-Engineering	COTS[3] Integration
Platform	Java	Java	Mainframe	Mainframe	Mixed
UML Experience	Yes	Yes	No	No	Yes
Status	Discontinued	In Progress	In Progress	In Progress	Completed
#Employees	4	2	1	2	3

design systems based on a standard language supported by tools (UML), and store textual information along with the design. Another advantage stated by participants was the ability to generate and re-generate stakeholder views whenever a design aspect changed. One advantage expected by the participants is to re-use the specifications and documentation in future projects.

3.2.2 UML and UML-Tooling Imply a Learning Curve

Solution Architects without prior experience in using UML or a UML-based modeling tool require time to familiarize themselves with both, the notation and the tool. This is particularly true for employees with little or no experience in object-oriented terminology, which is common for solution architects of mainframe systems. Participants with this background found the customized UML profile helpful, which provides platform-specific terminology (e.g. PLI-modules are indicated by UML components with the <<PLI>> stereotype applied).

Based on the participants' feedback, the time required becoming familiar with UML and the tooling was estimated to take approximately one week, on the job, however noting that 'substantially more time' is required to reach the productivity-level of their previous non-formal approach to specification.

3.2.3 Customized Training Curriculum Required

UML and tool training for the participants in the piloting projects was provided based on standard offerings by the tool vendor. A training session specific to TSDOC was held, conducted several times for different projects each.

The participants questioned the applicability of the vendor-provided tool and UML training in their particular project: the challenge is not seen in using a UML-based tool for system design, but the *application of UML in the scope of a particular design context and technology platform*. Therefore, a training curriculum tailored to Credit Suisse is currently under consideration.

---

[3] Commerical off-the-shelf product.

3.2.4 Need for Efficient Technical Support and Knowledge Sharing

All participants experienced problems while using the UML tool, ranging from uncertainty about expressing certain design constructs using UML, to technical failures such as the crashing of the tool or inability to re-open existing UML models.

The technical problems were reported to and resolved by Credit Suisse support staff. Questions regarding the application of UML were discussed in a bi-weekly workgroup were recent issues and proposed solutions were shared.

3.2.5 Increasing Precision in Specifications

It was particularly interesting to observe the need for discussing design questions, apparently triggered by UML: expressing a particular design aspect using UML - instead of a non-formal description or graphic - seems to raise design-related questions and drive a desire to be (more) precise. This increased awareness for preciseness is an encouraging sign to potentially improving design quality as experience grows and knowledge is shared. However, this assumption could not yet be verified.

3.2.6 Non-formal Content Still Valuable

In all projects, existing documentation had to be integrated with the UML models. While some of the content could be translated into UML (e.g. lists of components and adjacent interface specifications), other content had to be represented "as such" (e.g. textual descriptions of non-functional requirements).

4 Concluding Remarks

The approach described, TSDOC, implies that specifications and documentation of IT systems are based on UML models instead of non-formal documents. By means of an appropriate tool infrastructure for configuration management, specifications are kept an integral part of a system's releases. The UML models become the single source for multiple, stakeholder-specific views, thus reducing unwarranted redundancy. TSDOC further supports to leverage the benefits associated with collaborative development scenarios, co-located and offshore, namely by reduced ambiguity of specifications.

As first experiences at Credit Suisse indicate, the use of UML implies a learning curve, yet allow practitioners to be more precise than by using non-formal specifications. As a general implication for global software development, the major challenge remains to agree a common metamodel compliant to match stakeholder-specific reporting needs, and to institutionalize the use of UML across the organization and its partners. Institutionalization implies a customized curriculum, knowledge sharing among practitioners, and a sustained effort to support an efficient tool infrastructure.

References

1. IEEE: ANSI/IEEE Std 1471–2000 Recommended Practice for Architectural Description of Software-Intensive Systems (2000)
2. The Open Group: The Open Group Architectural Framework (TOGAF), http://www.opengroup.org/architecture/togaf

 3. Kruchten, P.B.: The 4+1 view model of architecture. IEEE Software 28(11), 42–50 (1995)
 4. Hill, R.: An ISO/IEC 42010 (IEEE Std 1471) Annotated Bilbiography, Version 1.5 (2008)
 5. Zachman, J.A.: A framework for information systems architecture. IBM Systems Journal 26(3), 276–292 (1987)
 6. Kruchten, P.B.: The Rational Unified Process: an introduction. Addison-Wesley, Reading (1999)
 7. Clements, P.C., Bachmann, F., Bass, L., Garlan, D., Ivers, J., Little, R., Nord, R., Stafford, J.: Documenting Software Architectures: views and beyond. Addison Wesley, Reading (2003)
 8. Egyed, A., Medvidovic, N.: Architectural Representation in UML with View Integration. In: 2nd International Conference on the Unified Modelling Language (October 1999)
 9. Hilliard, R.: Using the UML for Architectural Description. Springer, Heidelberg (1999)
10. Hofmeister, C., Nord, R.L., Soni, D.: Describing Software Architecture with UML. Siemens Corporate Research. Kluwer Academic Publishers, Dordrecht (1999)
11. Murer, S., Worms, C., Furrer, F.J.: Managed Evolution. Informatik-Spectrum. Springer, Heidelberg (2008)

The Role of Contracts in
Distributed Development

Martin Nordio[1], Roman Mitin[1], Bertrand Meyer[1], Carlo Ghezzi[2],
Elisabetta Di Nitto[2], and Giordano Tamburrelli[2]

[1] ETH Zurich, Switzerland
{Martin.Nordio,Roman.Mitin,Bertrand.Meyer}@inf.ethz.ch
[2] Politecnico di Milano, Italy
tambug@gmail.com, carlo.ghezzi@polimi.it, dinitto@elet.polimi.it

Abstract. Distributed software development raises new software engineering challenges resulting from the difficulty of making several teams
cooperate across different countries, time zones and cultures. These obstacles can lead to critical delays or even failures. One of the most effective techniques for overcoming them is to improve the quality of software
specifications. Our experience with a distributed software project in an
educational environment suggests that Design by Contract techniques
provide a promising solution.

Keywords: Software Requirements Specifications, Distributed Development, Interface Specifications, Contracts.

1 Specifications in Distributed Software Development

Whether outsourced [24] or not, todays software projects are ever more often
distributed: developed by two or more teams working in different locations.
Distributed software development poses new software engineering challenges;
previous work has, for example, analyzed how to adapt the old idea of "code
reviews" to this new setup [25]. Here we consider another difficulty of distributed
software development: how to mitigate the risk of *misunderstanding software
specifications*.

The case of particular interest is the sharing of specifications between a
"client" team which needs a certain functionality and a "supplier" team which
implements that functionality. We will present the use of Design by Contract
techniques [23,27] to express the specifications in a precise yet understandable
way, acceptable to both client and supplier teams.

Section 2 describes the source of the experiments described here: distributed
software projects involving teams from different universities. Section 3 presents
some of the typical problems encountered in the absence of a systematic approach
to specification. Section 4 solves these problems using contracts. Section 5 describes how our approach has been applied to distributed projects. Finally, we
present the results, related work, and the lessons learnt during the project.

O. Gotel, M. Joseph, and B. Meyer (Eds.): SEAFOOD 2009, LNBIP 35, pp. 117–129, 2009.
© Springer-Verlag Berlin Heidelberg 2009

2   Context of This Study

While some of the authors have applied the techniques described here in commercial distributed developments, the experience underlying this article is based on an academic effort rather than an industrial project.

For several years the Chair of Software Engineering at ETH Zurich has taught a course entitled *"Distributed and Outsourced Software Engineering"* or *DOSE*[1], which since 2007 has included a course project pursued in cooperation with other universities, most recently Politecnico di Milano (Italy), Odessa National Polytechnic University (Ukraine), the State University of Nizhny Novgorod (Russia), and University of Debrecen (Hungary). While each university retains its own course and organization, the project is shared: each project group includes teams from different universities. Specifically, each group in the current setup is made of three teams, each including two students from a given university. (This terminology is needed to understand the rest of the discussion: a *group* does the full project and is made of teams, each doing a part of the project; a *team* is made of students from one university, but a group involves teams from different universities.) All software is developed in Eiffel using the EiffelStudio Integrated Development Environment.

As a result of this project scheme, the students get to experience the challenges of true distributed development; they face the same difficulties as in a distributed project in industry, compounded by the specific constraints of a university environment. As an example of where an "academic" setup can in fact be tougher than an industrial one, the option of delaying the final delivery (an event that, although undesirable, often happens in industry) is not available: come rain or shine, the university administration requires instructors to give the students a grade at the end of the semester, a milestone that cannot be moved.

The course allows students to experience first-hand the tasks and challenges of modern software development, and learn critical skills; they consistently report that it is a richly rewarding experience. It also provides us with an opportunity to study issues of distributed development in a controlled environment.

One of these issues is the difficulty of communicating requirements. The difficulty is well known to anyone who has practiced industrial software development; it is also intuitively clear that project distribution increases it. Our experience provides concrete evidence of this phenomenon, as will now be described.

3   Specification-Related Errors in Distributed Development

An example from the 2007 session of the DOSE course [1] illustrates the specification risks of distributed development.

The project topic was the development of a system to analyze email postings of computer science events, in mailing lists such as the ECOOP list and SE

---

[1] Until 2006 the course was called "Software Engineering for Outsourced and Offshore Development".

World, to feed the Computer Science Event List (CSEL) [8], a Web page of Informatics Europe (http://events.informatics-europe.org). The automatic part of the system must identify key elements of a conference announcement, such as event name, event date and call for papers deadline, to prepare a CSEL entry. Since the identification cannot be perfect, the system includes a human editing step to correct any mistakes.

Figure 1 shows the Software Requirements Specification (SRS) as given to the students.

A. Scope
The system shall identify the elements of a call for paper posted in mailing lists, and feed them to the CSEL system by sending e-mails in the special format.

B. Definitions, Acronyms and Abbreviations
CSEL: Computer Science Event, *http://www.informatics-europe.org/cgi-bin/informatics_events.cgi*
Conference Name: Name of the event.
Conference Dates: Starting and ending dates of the event.
Abstract Deadline: The date for the abstract submission.
Submission Deadline: The date for the paper submission.
Conference Category: Kind of the event (symposium, conference, workshop, etc).

C. Product functions
The system shall
    C.1. Provide functionalities to extract the information of a conference from an e-mail (a text e-mail, no html);
    C.2. Report the extracted information in a graphical user interface (GUI);
    C.3. Allow modifying this information;
    C.4. Submit the information to the CSEL system by sending e-mails.

D. Specific requirements
    D.1. The system shall be able to extract the elements of a call for paper from text e-mails. The elements of a call for paper are the following: (1) Conference name, (2) Conference dates, (3) Abstract deadline, (4) Submission deadline, (5) Place where the conference takes place, (6) URL of the conference, (7) Conference sponsor, (8) Contact information, (9) Keywords of the conference, and (10) Conference category.
    D.2. The conference category is either *"Conference"* or *"Symposium"* or *"Workshop"* or *"Summer School"*.
    D.3. The system shall visualize conference information, and allow modifying it. The system shall feed the approved information by sending e-mail to *CSEL* as a comma separated list.
    D.4. All the elements from D.1 must be in the e-mail. If any of this information could not be extracted, the system shall add the keyword *NONE* in corresponding element.
    D.5. The system can send the e-mail only if at least all key elements have been extracted or introduced by the user. The key elements are: (1) conference name, (2) conference dates, (3) abstract deadline, (4) submission deadline, (5) place where the conference takes place, and (6) URL of the conference.

Fig. 1. Example Software Requirements Specification

The teaching team divided the system into three clusters (subsystems):

- *A - ANALYZE:* automatically extract the essential information.
- *B - BEFIT:* user interface for interactive correction.
- *C - COMBINE:* integration of components *A*, *B* and the CSEL website.

Correspondingly, each project group was divided into three teams, each from a given university, for example two teams performing task *A* and *B* in Zurich, and a team *C* in Odessa.

While undoubtedly not perfect, the requirements document of Figure 1 was written carefully and would appear to be clear enough. When given to teams working in different locations, however, it led to misunderstandings that the specification literature has analyzed [22]. In particular, the following problems arose. (We use the phrase "Team *A*" to mean "The team in charge of implementing cluster *A* in one of the groups," and similarly for other clusters. Different examples may involve different groups.)

Case 1. Team *A* implemented the abstract deadline using the date format *day.month.year* where *day*, *month*, and *year* are integers. Team *B* used a different format, with integers for the day and year but a string (such as "January" or "February") for the month. This misunderstanding, affecting the type of an attribute, caused a delay in the integration. It can be traced to a lack of precision of the specification (the SRS).

Case 2. Team *C* realized that the abstract submission deadline must always be earlier than the paper submission deadline. Thus, they checked this property before submitting the conference information to CSEL. If this property did not hold, an exception was triggered. Team *B*, in devising the user interface, did not check for this property and accepted any combination of dates. As a result, some combinations crashed the system. A similar problem happened to another group with the starting and the ending conference dates. The problem here is the specifications failure to state a requirement which appears necessary to someone trying to understand the system semantics.

Case 3. Team *A* understood that the category of a conference is "Conference" **or** "Symposium" **or** "Workshop" **or** "Summer School", where **or** is the usual, non-exclusive boolean disjunction. Team *B* interpreted it as an exclusive or. As a result, some test cases passed the checks performed in cluster *A* but not those of *B*, again triggering run-time exceptions and failure. The problem here is the lack of precision of natural language.

Case 4. The teams used a class called *EVENT* to model the notion of conference, but had slightly different interpretations of the semantics of this class. In the view of Team *C*, class *EVENT* only models conferences that satisfy basic validity constraints, such as the Call for Papers deadline appearing before the notification date. Teams *A* and *B* assumed that the class models any conference,even one with invalid information; they checked the validity of the information before submitting it to CSEL. These conflicting conventions were discovered late in the project and delayed integration. The problem in this case is not in the original requirements specification but in the lack of precision of module interface specifications produced during the design phase.

In this 2007 session of the DOSE course, no project succeeded in producing a system that could be actually deployed, although at least one came tantalizingly close; it was probably a week or two away from success but, as noted, there is no possibility of extension in a university course context. In our analysis the main reason for this result is the accumulation of specification issues such as the above, each small in itself but leading to mistakes and delays. That so many such issues could arise in a small system with a fairly straightforward specification gives an idea of the trouble insufficient specification techniques can cause in large industrial software developments.

4   Using Contracts to Avoid Specification Errors

Avoiding the kind of problems illustrated above involves technical and non-technical measures. As an example of the latter, it is always desirable to check the requirements for satisfaction of the properties listed in the IEEE Standard on Requirements specification [15], such as absence of ambiguity. Such goals are, however, quite general, and the standard does not specify how to achieve them and assess the results.

Using a *formal specification* technique would remove ambiguity and help achieve some of the other quality goals. A fully formal approach is, however, beyond the reach of most teams.

Design by Contract techniques retain some of the benefits of formal methods but are far easier to teach to developers who are competent software engineers (or, in our case, software engineering or computer science students) but have not necessarily received special formal methods training.

The basic idea of Design by Contract [23,27] is to attach partial but rigorous specifications to software elements: preconditions and postconditions for routines, and (in an object-oriented) invariants for classes. Design by Contract has applications to software construction, documentation, testing (in particular with the recent development of automatic testing tools such as AutoTest [26,5]), proper use of programming mechanisms such as inheritance and exception handling, and management. The application of most interest here is to the specification of module interfaces.

Specifications using Design by Contract use a subset of the programming language (typically Eiffel, but others have been proposed, such as Spec# [3] and JML [18,19]); assertions (contract) elements are boolean expressions, with some extensions such as the **old** notation in postconditions.

The class interface in Figure 2, expressed in Eiffel, describes the notion of event as managed in our example system.

Class *EVENT* relies on an auxiliary class *CATEGORY* (presented in Figure 3).

The actual class texts will contain implementations of the features involved (*submit_to_csel* etc.); the above are interface specifications, which can be written first and then refined into the implementations, or extracted automatically

```
1 indexing
      description : "Technical events as managed in the CSEL."
3
   class
5     EVENT


7 feature    -- Basic operations


9    submit_to_csel
                    -- Submit the conference information by sending an e mail.
11      require
             valid_conferences :   starting_date . earlier_than  (ending_date)
13           valid_deadlines :   abstract_deadline . earlier_than  (paper_deadline)
        do
15      end


17 feature    -- Implementation


19   name: STRING
     starting_date :  DATE
21   ending_date: DATE
     abstract_deadline :  DATE
23   paper_deadline: DATE
     place ,  url ,  sponsor ,  keywords: STRING
25   a_category :  CATEGORY


27 invariant
          category_status :   a_category . is_conference  xor
29                             a_category . is_symposium  xor
                               a_category . is_workshop    xor
31                             a_category . is_summer_school


33 end
```

Fig. 2. Interface Specification of a Class *EVENT*

(by tools of the development environment) from these implementations if they already exist.

Class *EVENT* as given serves as a precise specification of the notion of event, avoiding the errors and ambiguities that occurred during the 2007 project development cited above. Note in particular how the class invariant expresses, through the use of the exclusive-or operator **xor**, that the different categories of event are exclusive. The precondition (**require** clause) of procedure *submit_to_csel* states validity requirements: the starting date must precede the ending date, and the deadline for abstracts must precede the deadline for papers.

```
 1 indexing
       description : "Conference categories."
 3
   class
 5    CATEGORY

 7 feature    -- Status report

 9    is_conference : BOOLEAN
                   -- Does this category represent conferences?
11        do
          end
13
      is_symposium: BOOLEAN
15                -- Does this category represent symposiums?
          do
17        end

19    is_workshop: BOOLEAN
                  -- Does this category represent workshops?
21        do
          end
23
      is_summer_school: BOOLEAN
25                -- Does this category represent summer schools?
          do
27        end

29 end
```

Fig. 3. Interface Specification of a Class *CATEGORY*

5   Improving the Project Setup

The preceding example suggests that a systematic use of contracts can provide considerable help towards solving the specification and communication issues that plague distributed projects. We used the 2008 session of the DOSE course to assess this conjecture.

A number of characteristics changed between the 2007 and 2008 sessions. DOSE 2007 [1] had, as noted, the CSEL system as the project theme. In 2007 the project, developed over 11 weeks out of the semesters 13, was divided into four phases:

- *Phase 1:* Write specification of each cluster (4 weeks).
- *Phase 2:* Revise and consolidate the specification into one project document; develop interface specification using contracts (3 weeks).
- *Phase 3:* Implement clusters (2 weeks).
- *Phase 4:* Test system (2 weeks).

As indicated for Phase 2, students were encouraged to use contracts, but this was only a recommendation. Faced with the difficulties mentioned earlier, students gradually realized the importance of precise specifications and started applying contracts more systematically. In the end, however, the delay in applying these techniques made it impossible to integrate the results into a deployable system.

DOSE 2008 [2] used a different project. We took advantage of the announcement of a competition in conjunction with the 2009 International Conference on Software Engineering (ICSE): the SCORE project competition [32]. Specifically, we chose one of the topics offered in the SCORE competition: "BTW" [28], a system to provide advice to someone planning a trip to a city. As in 2007, we divided the project into three clusters to be handled by different teams within a group; the *BTW* clusters were:

- *Cluster 1 - SYST:* GUI and overall organization of the *BTW* system
- *Cluster 2 - GEO:* Interface with *GIS* information and Traffic
- *Cluster 3 - PLAN:* Route planning and advice

and typical group configurations were:

- (1) Zurich - (2) Nizhny Novgorod - (3) Milano
- (1) Debrecen - (2) Milano - (3) Zurich
- (1) Milano - (2) Zurich - (3) Odessa

The problem domain made it possible to take advantage of an existing system for city modeling and route planning, the Traffic library [20], developed at ETH for the purposes of our introductory programming course [16].

While the overall setup was similar to the 2007 session, we changed a number of elements in light of the lessons learned. We started the project earlier, so that it could use 13 weeks out of the semesters 14. Recognizing the importance and difficulty of the specification phase, we extended it to 5 weeks and simplified the process by bringing the number of phases to three:

- *Phase 1:* Write specification of each cluster (4 weeks).
- *Phase 2:* Revise and consolidate the specification into one project document; develop interface specifications using contracts (5 weeks).
- *Phase 3:* Implement clusters (4 weeks).

We gave much more precise and prescriptive recommendations to students:

- They were told to get in touch with the other teams in the very first week; this avoided communication issues and simplified the revision of the requirements document.
- We introduced a code review to improve the interface specification.
- Students had to implement the projects in two cycles, which helped to find integrations problems earlier.
- We strongly encouraged them to commit the code daily, and to define and apply precise commit rules (such as permitting commit *only if the code has been compiled and tested*).

Most importantly, we made the inclusion of contract interface specifications mandatory in the specifications.

6   Results

The results of the 2008 projects confirmed the usefulness of the measures described above. The final result of the implemented projects was good: the systems were integrated and the three clusters worked in the same system. The specification of the interfaces was improved, and contracts helped to document and understand the interfaces.

To obtain the students perspective we asked them to fill a feedback questionnaire, which most of them (95%) did.

Most of the students think that contracts helped to develop the project. We wanted to know how much effort the contracts required. Table 1 shows the hour/person per team expended in developing the requirements documents with interface specification using contracts. In average, the development of contracts took 22.2% of the time used in the requirement phase.

The results of the experience show that contracts were key to develop distributed projects. The use of contracts in SRS have been useful not only to avoid misunderstandings but also to specify the interaction between subsystems. Projects that defined good interfaces using contracts have been able to deploy, and produce a final system. On the other side, projects that have not specified the interfaces properly have failed to produce a final system.

To go beyond such assessments, we intend to perform a more objective measurement of the specification effort as part of DOSE 2009.

Table 1. Effort expended developing requirements documents and interfaces with contracts

	T1	T2	T3	T4	T5	T6	T7	T8	T9	T10	T11	T12	**Average**
Person/hours SRS (without contracts)	35	64.6	116	108	39	82	27	34	19	89	28	22	**55.3**
Person/hours writing contracts	20	15	20	20	8	30	8	4	20	30	7	8	**15.8**
Percentage in writing contracts	36.3	18.8	14.7	15.6	17.0	26.7	22.8	10.5	51.2	25.2	20	26.6	**22.2**

7   Related Work

Industry and academia have been interested in distributed development. Lessons learnt on educational experiences have been reported [9,7,4]. Gotel et al. [9,10] describe the lessons learned from the development of a project across three globally distributed educational institutions. The institutions that participated in that project were Pace University (US), University of Delhi (India), and Institute of Technology of Cambodia (Cambodia). They discuss the problems faced in the projects such as communication (with a twelve hours time difference), project planning, and cultural aspects. A similar experience is described by Damian et al. [7]. They report on the teaching experience developing software requirements specifications in geographically distributed software development with three universities (located in Canada, Australia, and Italy), focusing on the times zones and the cultural differences. These works focus on how to teach a course in distributed software development. However, they do not cover how to improve software requirements specifications. A deeper description of existing works concerning global development and educational experiences is beyond the scope of this paper and can be found in [4,12,13,29].

Corriveau [6] indentifies the key properties that a contract between the parties involved in outsourcing must satisfy. These properties are expressed with a model, and this model must be testable, executable, and abstract. This model is used to test the quality of the developed project, but it does not help to understand the system under development. Our approach is used to solve the problems of potential misunderstandings in software requirements specifications, and to improve them. The use of contracts brings the same properties: testable, executable, and abstraction. Meyer et al. [21] have described our first experience in distributed software development, DOSE 2007. They described the experiences of software engineering projects in local and distributed developments. However, the role of contracts in software requirements specification is not discussed.

Sutherland et al. [33] report the industrial experience of developing a distributed project with two companies: SirsiDynix (Utah, US) and StarSoft Development Laboratories (St. Petersburg, Russia). They analyze and recommend best practices for globally distributed agile teams. They report that distributed teams can be as productive as a small collocated team.

Concerning program specifications, many existing works address this issue from different points of view and with different goals. The fact that natural language specifications lead to unsatisfactory and ambiguous specifications is well known and widely accepted. This issue becomes crucial in distributed or global development settings. Nevertheless, specifications based on natural language descriptions even if supported by diagrams (e.g., UML [34]) are still widely adopted in industrial development. Consequently, several existing approaches aim at supporting software development with specifications based on natural language [14,31], however, the most promising techniques rely on the adoption of formalisms.

Languages such as Alloy [17] can be used to solve the problems of ambiguous specifications. However, the specification is completely detached from the source code of the program leading to a traceability gap among code and its specification. Moreover, concerning UML, it is important to notice the difference among writing contracts in Eiffel and writing constraints in the Object Constraint Language (OCL) [34]. First of all, the former approach offers a precise and non ambiguous semantics conversely to the UML object constraint language (several approaches addressed this issue, e.g. [30]). Secondly, OCL suffers from a traceability gap between the specifications and the implementation, while our approach does not.

The Java Modeling Language (JML) [18,19] is a behavioral interface specification language that can be used to specify the behavior of Java modules. It combines the design by contract approach of Eiffel and the model-based specification approach of the Larch family of interface specification languages [11]. Although the approach is similar to Eiffel contracts, specifications in JML are not part of the Java language. Furthermore, Spec# [3] extends C# with formal specifications. In our approach, the specifications are not restricted to any programming language, thus JML and Spec# can be used to specify the interfaces of distributed projects.

8   Conclusions and DOSE 2009

We have presented an approach to improve software requirements specifications by integrating contracts to SRS. To measure the results of this approach, we have developed several distributed projects. Contracts have helped to solve the problems of misunderstanding and underspecification in SRS. The use of contracts brings the advantages of automatic testing and better system documentation. Although the experiments were performed in an academic environment, we believe that the results are also interesting to industrial software developers.

Since the distributed projects in DOSE 2007 and DOSE 2008 have been an interesting experience, we plan to continue this experiment in 2009. So far, we have developed projects with two and three geographically different locations. During DOSE 2009 we have observed that projects distributed in two locations have less overhead in communication and development than projects developed in three locations. However, we have not executed any empirical study that shows what is the overhead. Next year, we plan to analyze this overhead in communication and development when projects are distributed in two, three, and four locations. If you are a member of an academic institution and would like to be part of DOSE 2009, please contact us to discuss and organize your participation.

Acknowledgements

We would like to thank all the people involved in DOSE 2007 and DOSE 2008 especially Dr. Peter Kolb, Prof. Viktor Gergel, Andrey Zaychikov, Lajos Kollár, Prof. Juhász István, and Prof. Victor Krissilov; to the students who worked hard and gave us useful feedback; to Scott West for reviewing and providing helpful comments on drafts of this paper.

References

1. DOSE 2007 (2007),
   http://se.ethz.ch/teaching/2007-f/outsourcing-0273/index.html
2. DOSE 2008 (2008),
   http://se.ethz.ch/teaching/2008-h/dose-0273/index.html

3. Barnett, M., Leino, K.R.M., Schulte, W.: The Spec# programming system: An overview. In: Barthe, G., Burdy, L., Huisman, M., Lanet, J.-L., Muntean, T. (eds.) CASSIS 2004. LNCS, vol. 3362, pp. 49–69. Springer, Heidelberg (2005)
4. Bruegge, B., Dutoit, A.H., Kobylinski, R., Teubner, G.: Transatlantic project courses in a university environment. In: 7th Asia-Pacific Software Engineering Conference (APSEC 2000), pp. 30–37 (2000)
5. Ciupa, I., Leitner, A., Oriol, M., Meyer, B.: ARTOO: Adaptive Random Testing for Object-Oriented Software. In: Proceedings of the 30th International Conference on Software Engineering 2008 (ICSE 2008) (May 2008)
6. Corriveau, J.P.: Testable Requirements for Offshore Outsourcing. In: Meyer, B., Joseph, M. (eds.) SEAFOOD 2007. LNCS, vol. 4716, pp. 27–43. Springer, Heidelberg (2007)
7. Damian, D., Lanubile, F., Mallardo, T.: Investigating IBIS in a Distributed Educational Environment: the Design of a Case Study. In: Workshop on Distributed Software Engineering, vol. 1 (2005)
8. Computer Science Event, http://www.informatics-europe.org/cgi-bin/informatics_events.cgi
9. Gotel, O., Kulkarni, V., Neak, L.C., Scharff, C., Seng, S.: Introducing Global Supply Chains into Software Engineering Education. In: Meyer, B., Joseph, M. (eds.) SEAFOOD 2007. LNCS, vol. 4716, pp. 44–58. Springer, Heidelberg (2007)
10. Gotel, O., Kulkarni, V., Scharff, C., Neak, L.: Students as Partners and Students as Mentors: An Educational Model for Quality Assurance in Global Software Development. In: Berkling, K., Joseph, M., Meyer, B., Nordio, M. (eds.) SEAFOOD 2008. LNBIP, vol. 16. Springer, Heidelberg (2009)
11. Guttag, J.V., Horning, J.J., Garl, S.J., Jones, K.D., Modet, A., Wing, J.M.: Larch: languages and tools for formal specification. Texts and Monographs in Computer Science (1993)
12. Hawthorne, M.J., Perry, D.E.: Software engineering education in the era of outsourcing, distributed development, and open source software: challenges and opportunities. In: International Conference on Software Engineering, vol. 27, p. 643. Springer, Heidelberg (2005)
13. Herbsleb, J.D., Moitra, D.: Global software development. IEEE Software 18(2), 16–20 (2001)
14. Holt, A.: Formal verification with natural language specifications: guidelines, experiments and lessons so far. South African Computer Journal, 253–257 (1999)
15. IEEE: IEEE Recommended Practice for Software Requirements Specifiations. IEEE Std 830 (1998)
16. Introduction to Programming (Einführung in die Programmierung) - Chair of Software Engineering - ETH Zurich, http://se.ethz.ch/teaching/2008-h/eprog-0001/index.html
17. Jackson, D.: Alloy: a lightweight object modelling notation. ACM Transactions on Software Engineering and Methodology (TOSEM) 11(2), 256–290 (2002)
18. Leavens, G., Baker, A., Ruby, C.: JML: A notation for detailed design. Kluwer International Series in Engineering and Computer Science, pp. 175–188. Kluwer Academic Publishers, Dordrecht (1999)
19. Leavens, G.T., Baker, A.L., Ruby, C.: Preliminary design of JML: A behavioral interface specification language for Java. ACM SIGSOFT Software Engineering Notes 31(3), 1–38 (2006)
20. Traffic Library, http://traffic.origo.ethz.ch/

21. Meyer, B., Piccioni, M.: The allure and risks of a deployable software engineering project. In: Proceedings of the 21st IEEE-CS Conference on Software Engineering Education and Training (2008)
22. Meyer, B.: On formalism in specifications. IEEE Software 2(1), 6–26 (1985)
23. Meyer, B.: Object-Oriented Software Construction, 2nd edn. Prentice-Hall, Englewood Cliffs (1997)
24. Meyer, B.: The unspoken revolution in software engineering. IEEE Computer 39(1), 121–124 (2006)
25. Meyer, B.: Design and Code Reviews in the Age of the Internet. In: Berkling, K., Joseph, M., Meyer, B., Nordio, M. (eds.) SEAFOOD 2008. LNBIP, vol. 16. Springer, Heidelberg (2009)
26. Meyer, B., Ciupa, I., Leitner, A., Liu, L.L.: Automatic testing of object-oriented software. In: van Leeuwen, J., Italiano, G.F., van der Hoek, W., Meinel, C., Sack, H., Plášil, F. (eds.) SOFSEM 2007. LNCS, vol. 4362, pp. 114–129. Springer, Heidelberg (2007)
27. Meyer, B. (ed.): ISO/ECMA Eiffel standard (Standard ECMA-367: Eiffel: Analysis, Design and Programming Language) (June 2006), http://www.ecma-international.org/publications/standards/Ecma-367.htm
28. BTW Project, http://score.elet.polimi.it/projects.html
29. Richardson, I., Milewski, A.E., Mullick, N., Keil, P.: Distributed development: an education perspective on the global studio project. In: ICSE 2006: Proceedings of the 28th international conference on Software engineering, pp. 679–684. ACM, New York (2006)
30. Richters, M., Gogolla, M.: On formalizing the UML object constraint language OCL. In: Ling, T.-W., Ram, S., Li Lee, M. (eds.) ER 1998. LNCS, vol. 1507, pp. 449–464. Springer, Heidelberg (1998)
31. Saeki, M., Horai, H., Enomoto, H.: Software development process from natural language specification. In: ICSE 1989: Proceedings of the 11th international conference on Software engineering (1989)
32. SCORE, http://score.elet.polimi.it/
33. Sutherland, J., Viktorov, A., Blount, J., Puntikov, N.: Distributed scrum: Agile project management with outsourced development teams. In: HICSS 1940, Hawaii International Conference on Software Systems (2007)
34. UML, http://www.uml.org/

Managing Communication among Geographically Distributed Teams: A Brazilian Case

Ana Carina M. Almeida[1,2], Ivaldir H. de Farias Junior[1],
and Pedro Jorge de S. Carneiro[1,2]

[1] Federal University of Pernambuco (UFPE) – Informatics Center
Recife – PE – Brasil
{acma2,ihfj,pjsc}@cin.ufpe.br
[2] Centro de Estudos e Sistemas Avançados do Recife (C.E.S.A.R)
Rua Bione, 220 – Bairro do Recife – CEP 50030-390
Recife – PE – Brasil
{ana.almeida,pedro.santana}@cesar.org.br

Abstract. The growing demand for qualified professionals is making software companies opt for distributed software development (DSD). At the project conception, communication and synchronization of information are critical factors for success. However problems such as time-zone difference between teams, culture, language and different development processes among sites could difficult the communication among teams. In this way, the main goal of this paper is to describe the solution adopted by a Brazilian team to improve communication in a multisite project environment. The purposed solution was based on the best practices described in the literature, and the communication plan was created based on the infrastructure needed by the project. The outcome of this work is to minimize the impact of communication issues in multisite projects, increasing productivity, good understanding and avoiding rework on code and document writing.

Keywords: Communication, Distributed Software Development.

1 Introduction

Over the last decades, globalization has brought significant impacts to software development and management processes. Economic forces realized major investments to convert local markets in to global ones, increasing the significance of Distributed Software Development (DSD) in organizations today [1], [2].

There are many reasons why an organization should consider adopting a DSD model, including low-cost advantages, access to a local expertise in order to satisfy global demands, accelerate software development regarding market needs (time-to-market), round-the-clock working, and also being close to the customer, in order to properly understand their needs and business [1], [2], [3], [4], [5]. However, the adoption of DSD approaches introduces new challenges in Software Engineering area, such as, temporal, geographical and cultural distances. These challenges affect the

O. Gotel, M. Joseph, and B. Meyer (Eds.): SEAFOOD 2009, LNBIP 35, pp. 130–135, 2009.
© Springer-Verlag Berlin Heidelberg 2009

whole development team, but mainly the project managers who need to synchronize their activities and communication among different sites, with different time zones, cultural aspects, and usually different development process [1], [2], [5].

In order to have aligned information among sites it is required to elaborate a communication plan which intends to support the communication and management of development activities. Unfortunately, the current available quality models for software development, such as CMMI, MPS.BR, ISO 12207, ISO 15504, do not go deeply on DSD context, so there is a lack of best practices focus on multisite development.

For this reason, the purpose of this paper is to describe the solution we found to improve communication in a Brazilian multisite project that have started two years ago and already had more than nine releases published. To accomplish this, we talk about the artifacts, tools and also mention the lessons learned and future works for improving communication in distributed teams.

This paper is organized as follows: Section 2 gives a brief introduction about managing communication among DSD; Section 3 explains the Communication Plan; Section 4 presents the lessons learned and Section 5 shows the conclusions of this research.

2 Managing Communication among Geographically Distributed Teams

In order to have success in developing systems it is required to elaborate and track planning, risks, dependencies, tasks, estimates, team performance and other factors [6]. According to Mulcahy [7], the project communication is the main challenge of the project manager. It is critical to structure and control communication between team, stakeholders and company areas in order to achieve the project main purpose [8].

Some researches indicates that using DSD in a project increases the communication complexity and introduces new challenges, because the teams work in different time zones and have possible differences in culture and language [3], [4], [6], [8].

Considering this, in 2008, Farias Junior [9] did an exploratory study considering a lot of DSD projects and noticed that the main communication issues in DSD are: (i) overage formal communication, (ii) non adequate structure to support communication among distributed teams, (iii) lacking of face to face meetings and (iv) lack of knowledge about cultural aspects of the other sites. In his work he also purpose some good practices to minimize communication issues in DSD projects.

In addition, it was noticed that in the last decade, there are few research groups that treat this, such as, MuNNDoS [1], DiSEN, and other authors, like, Carmel [4] and Damian [10], but they do not specify what is needed to be done to have sufficient communication in multisite development. For sure, specific quality models for DSD can be very helpful for software industry.

3 Communication Plan

The communication plan and artifacts that we are describing below intended to improve communication among multisite development. We had 5 sites in Brazilian territories: 2 sites in the northeast area and 3 in the southeast. Each team has at least 10 system engineers. The sponsor was localized in the United States, they outsourced the project.

The project aimed to develop a Software Development Kit (SDK) for different Mobile Platforms. We used different technologies to implement this application. The site 01 was responsible for creating a framework on top of the Eclipse Platform in an extensible way and also defining together the other sites a set of features and standards in order to reuse the main core components among sites.

This section describes which tools were used to align communication among the development sites and also to allow projects output integration.

To reach such objectives, Mulcanhy [7] recommends elaborating the project communication planning. This artifact describes the project stakeholders, which information needs to be aligned among teams and the frequency and technology used to perform the communication between the development teams and the project sponsor.

According to Kerzner [8], it is important to identify what needs to be communicated and which site needs information, the best approach of communication to use, teams responsibility definition and which is the proper time to communicate with them.

Table 1 describes the different ways used to share information among project stakeholders as an example of a communication plan.

Table 1. Communication Plan example

Receiver	Necessity / Information Type	Description	Periodicity	Collecting method
Sponsor, Sites 02, 03, 04, 05	Responses to issues, questions or doubts submitted to the framework mailing list.	Issues, questions or clarifications submitted to the mailing list related to the framework or the other development sites.	Daily	Through the framework mailing list.
Sponsor, Sites 02, 03, 04, 05	Relevant information about the framework project that must be shared among teams	Align information among all team sites.	Biweekly	Framework biweekly meetings.

We used different ways for communicating among teams. The most commons were email, instant message, mailing list, wiki and conference calls. We also had twice a year, face to face meetings.

Below we are summarizing each resource that was used for improving communication among distributed teams.

– The Kick-off Meeting

We used the kick-off meeting to align information about the project scope with the whole team every beginning of the release. We elaborated a presentation and sent it to the whole team some hours before the meeting. During the meeting, we shared the presentation with all those who attended by Netmeeting tool.

The main scope of the presentation was: release purpose, scope, and planning, the baseline dates, the risks, assumptions and the team responsibility regarding the release.

– Biweekly Meeting

We had at least two meetings per month with all stakeholders in order to align goal, priorities, changes on scope, and any other item needed to be discussed.

We scheduled this meeting for the whole year checking the stakeholders' agenda. We sent friendly reminder emails 3 days before each the meeting. We also used this opportunity to encourage all team sites to contribute with the meeting agenda. Primarily, we posted the preliminary agenda at Wiki site, and then all team members were able to update the agenda including any desired item to be discussed.

Normally the agenda main topics were: Team Focal Points, Roles and Responsibilities among teams, Communication Process, Release Planning, Next Release Scope, Architectural Components, Impacts, Risks and Issues, CCB Session, Questions and Comments.

– Project Portal

We created a unique repository to share all information about the project in order to make it available in an easy way to all.

The Project Portal is a collaborative web site that provides all necessary information for the development teams and guarantees that each team knows the main goals of the project.

The main information stored there is the project focal points (email and rule), framework main goals, technical tips and trips (e.g. how to extend the framework), the release planning, milestones and scope. Support information was also available, such as, project mailing list, wiki, developer guide, contribution and compliance processes, deliverables, release dates, bug tracking, and other resources.

– Wiki

We included all technical documentation on wiki site, so the developers could help to write and share information about the framework architecture with others. It is a very interesting approach, because all sites were responsible to improve the documentation, contributing with the topic that they have more knowledge or feel more self-confident to document.

4 Lessons Learned

It was verified that the Project Portal creation improved the communication among development teams. Part of this achievement was because all teams were stimulated to collaborate, sharing information, like, teams' features schedule and release dates. In that way, the Project Portal improved the visibility of other teams, creating a unified product vision that could even help in their features negotiation with the sponsors.

Regarding the contribution and compliance verification processes, it was noticed that they improved the spirit of a single team, no matter where these were. In addition, it was observed that by adopting those processes the number of problems related to differences in the interface appearance, and system behaviors among products decreased significantly.

Regarding synchronous communication, conference calls were used by demand through a toll free number. In order to privilege all sites, it is recommended to schedule the meetings considering all sites time zones. Besides, it is also important to verify if all teams are comfortable with the meeting time.

In the same way, it was noticed the importance of establishing the meeting duration and align it with the attendees for how long each topic has to be discussed. Another helpful practice was to share the created presentation with the teams some hours before the meeting. These practices helped everyone come focused and prepared to discuss the highlighted subjects. During these meetings, open ended questions were used in order to check if the attendees understood the context. In order to share all decision makings in a quick manner, all team members' were reported through a short summary, called meeting minutes. These were sent to the mailing list and were also available in the project wiki.

As mentioned in section 3, the project mailing list was frequently used to discuss technical aspects and to communicate team's vacation and national holidays. Another simple but very helpful aspect we noticed was that as the mailing list stored a lot of useful information, it was usually used as an information retrieval tool for, for example, searching who made the decision or why it was made.

To avoid issues related to information update and accuracy, we decided to use at the same time a Project Portal and a Wiki. The decision to use both of them was made because they were used to achieve different goals. The first one was used to store static content (the content that does not change frequently) that can be updated by the administrator. For example, the development process that needs to be approved by the stakeholders. The second one was used to store dynamic content. By this way, the Wiki was used to store technical related content, for example, the Developer Guide.

Last by not least, a very helpful good practice was the use of ambassadors (people who travel between sites). This approach helped a lot to establish trust and cohesion between the teams and sponsors.

5 Conclusions

The nature of the global business environment has led companies to take advantage of benefits brought on by globalization. It is possible to understand what each region has to offer the best in terms of comparative advantages, either in terms of cost (human resources), quality, agility, less time-zone differences, policies, incentives, training, and number of people available.

On the other hand it is important to understand the challenges which this approach introduces. The goal of this research was to improve and align communication among distributed teams.

The research results and lessons learned confirmed that it was possible to mitigate communication risks and avoid project issues establishing simple infra-structure, aligning expectation and making the project information available for all. It was also important to motivate the team members to participate of whole process, contributing with the information improvement.

References

1. Audy, J.N., Prikladnicki, R.: Desenvolvimento Distribuído de Software, Rio de Janeiro, Brasil. Elsevier, Amsterdam (2008)
2. Agerfalk, P.J., Fitzgerald, B., Holmström, H., Lings, B., Lundell, B., Conchúir, E.O.: A Framework for Considering Opportunities and Threats in Distributed Software Development. In: International Workshop on Distributed Software Development, pp. 47–61 (2005)

3. Damian, D., Zowghi, D.: The impact of stakeholders? Geographical distribution on managing requirements in a multi-site organization. In: RE, pp. 319–330 (2002)
4. Carmel, E.: Global Software Teams – Collaborating Across Borders and Time-Zones. Prentice Hall, USA
5. James, D.H., Audris, M., Thomas, A.F., Rebecca, E.G.: Distance, dependencies, and delay in a global collaboration. ACM, Computer Supported Cooperative Work, Philadelphia (2000)
6. Liang, H.: Distributed Software Development. Leading Edge Forum
7. Mulcahy, R.: Preparatório para o Exame de PMP. 3ª Edição. RMC Publications, Inc. (2007)
8. Kerzner, H.: Project Management – A System Approach to Planning, Scheduling, and Controling, 8th edn
9. Farias Jr., I.H.: Uma Proposta de Boas Práticas do Processo de Comunicação para Projetos de Desenvolvimento Distribuído de Software. Dissertação de Mestrado, CIn - UFPE, Pernambuco (2008)
10. Damian, D., Zowghi, D.: The impact of stakeholders' geographical distribution on requirements engineering in a multi-site development organization. In: Proc. of the 10th IEEE Int'l Conference on Requirements Engineering (RE 2002), Essen, Germany, pp. 319–328 (2002)

Author Index

Printed in the United States
By Bookmasters

Printed in the United States
By Bookmasters